Comparative Law

COMPARATIVE LAW SERIES

Michael L. Corrado, Series Editor
UNIVERSITY OF NORTH CAROLINA
SCHOOL OF LAW

Comparative Law
An Introduction

Edited

by

Vivian Grosswald Curran

Carolina Academic Press
Durham, North Carolina

ISBN: 0-89089-730-1
LCCN: 2002101292

Carolina Academic Press
700 Kent Street
Durham, North Carolina 27701
Telephone (919) 489-7486
Fax (919) 493-5668
www.cap-press.com

Printed in the United States of America

For Roger, Rob, and Charlie

Contents

Contributors

Vivian Grosswald Curran is Professor of Law, University of Pittsburgh.

William Bragg Ewald is Professor of Law and Philosophy, University of Pennsylvania.

E. Allan Farnsworth is the Alfred McCormack Professor of Law, Columbia University.

Lon L. Fuller was the Carter Professor of General Jurisprudence, Harvard University.

Bernhard Großfeld is Emeritus Professor of Law, University of Münster.

Blanche Grosswald is Assistant Professor of Social Work, Rutgers University

Comparative Law

I. Introduction

In most European languages, whether Romance, Germanic or Slavic, law and comparative law are referred to as sciences. For example, in French, legal research commonly is described as *recherches scientifiques;* in German, the term *wissenschaftlich* is used, generally translated in English as "scientific;" and in Russian the same is true. Since the term "science" tends to have broader connotations in those languages than in English, it would be incorrect to conclude that French, German and Russian, among others, portray law as a science analogous to physics, chemistry or mathematics. Similarly, when we use the term "science" in phrases like "political science" or "the social sciences," we presumably do not mean to portray those fields as equivalent in all relevant ways to the natural sciences.

On the other hand, the widespread tendency to juxtapose law and science reflects an issue of concern and importance to the legal field: namely, how reliable is law? What is the relation between law and truth? Can law pretend to truth or at least to some truths? Can its tenets be verified? Is law merely or largely historical happenstance? Worse, is it, as some believe, reducible to the dictates of the powerful imposed on the powerless?

To the extent that we associate law with science, we may hold and convey the hope that objectivity resides in law. Objectivity implies impartiality, and impartiality implies lack of arbitrariness, fairness and justice. Since laws can affect human life in dramatic ways, such as imprisonment and, in some countries, even death through capital punishment, what can justify law if law is not objectively, scientifically, verifiably justifiable? To the extent that we concede arbitrariness as an element of law, do we not forgo the justification for imposing its strictures on members of society?

An examination of these issues in the legal field in general is beyond the scope of this small book on comparative law. Issues of truth, verifiability and purpose are, however, also vital to the field of comparative law. The purposes animating comparatists are many

3

and varied, and views as to the presumed nature of law itself influence comparatists in forming their projects and in interpreting their results. For example, if laws either do or should reflect universal human needs and attributes, then comparative law might be a way of discovering objectively verifiable human commonalities. Out of such a study, one could hope to compile a body of universal laws. This was the idea of many comparatists in the past. If, on the other hand, human universals are few and far between, and people have culturally determined differences that represent fundamental, distinctive concerns, desires and attributes, then the comparatist's project would focus, rather, on identifying the characteristics of different peoples and different legal cultures, without aspiring to develop a set of universal legal ideals.

Of course, a project also is possible somewhere in between the ideal of pervasive universal laws and the belief that no common laws can be adapted to all humankind. There may be some universal human characteristics amenable to some shared, unifying rules of law. Although few in number, such laws nevertheless might be fundamental. One might think in this context of a law against torture. Highly diverse as the countries of the world are today, few or none would advocate torture, even among those which nevertheless might practice it. One must be careful, however, before assuming that all peoples would contemplate the same concept when proscribing torture. Disagreement assuredly would arise in different cultures as to where the defining lines should be drawn. For example, amputating the hand of a convicted thief might be decried as torture in one country while viewed as just retribution in another.

The twentieth century saw great political and human turmoil, producing reactions often passionately held, but sometimes mutually incompatible. On the one hand, many scholars in the second half of the century, as well as many citizens of nations around the world, looked to the rule of law as an antidote against the horrors perpetrated by totalitarian rulers during the first half of the century. On the other hand, the unsurpassed trauma and turmoil of the first half of the century often involved the abuse and distortion of laws, with a cynical undermining of law's role in society. This created a reaction among some scholars and citizens that took the form of skepticism towards law, particularly with respect to law's potential in times of economic and political crises.

The beginning of a new century and millennium finds us at the cusp of a new socio-political era, examining and reexamining the roles and potential uses of comparative legal studies. Ours is a world undergoing technological revolutions that have brought the globe together as never before, and that inevitably seem destined to continue to result in increased global contacts and confrontations. In this ever-shrinking, globalized world, what does it mean to compare? Does comparison necessarily imply judging other systems, other ways of living? To what extent should comparative legal analysis strive to unify or to differentiate? Should it merely identify? Can the attempt to identify and describe ever separate itself completely from judgment, and can judgment ever separate itself completely from bias?

This book will attempt to convey potentials and limitations of the field of comparative legal analysis, and some perceptions of what comparative law is and should seek to be. A central, underlying thesis is that the comparative enterprise is at the heart of all analysis, and of all understanding. Consequently, to engage in comparative legal analysis is to gain access to more than the substance of what one compares: it is also to observe and gain insights into some of the processes by which reasoning and intellectual discovery occur.

Comparative legal analysis has had a rich and lustrous history. Its meanderings have followed the routes of human strivings, foibles and inspirations. Our perceptions of comparative law's uses are ever amenable to modification. This book does not expect or hope to provide answers so much as to signal, and perhaps even open, paths of inquiry.

II. Comparative Law in the United States: The Second Half of the Twentieth Century

1. *Introduction*

Comparative law became an academic field and a part of the curriculum of most United States law schools in the second half of the twentieth century. The essay below describes the development of comparative law in the United States, and offers some historical explanations for assumptions long unchallenged in the field that more recently have been questioned and revisited. In the author's view, comparative law developed in the shadows of the holocaust, and that catastrophe indirectly shaped the directions comparative legal analysis followed in the United States.

2. *A Universalist Tradition*

(a) Vivian Grosswald Curran, *Cultural Immersion, Difference and Categories in U.S. Comparative Law*
46 American Journal of Comparative Law 43, 66–78; 78–83 (1998)

The dominant theory of the modern era of comparative law has been the conscious, articulated intent to identify unifying elements and to discount differentiating ones. The authors of a prominent book on comparative law, much used in the United States, advocate a functionalist perspective for comparative legal studies, and see that objective as being furthered by findings of similarity and impeded by findings of difference: "Every legal system in the world is open to the same questions and subject to the same standards, even countries of different social structures or different stages of development." n76

The authors, Zweigert and Kötz, explicitly articulate that their aim is to avoid finding differences. They prioritize similarity by having as their recommended point of departure for the comparative enterprise a *"praesumptio similitudinis,"* n77 which they define as "a presumption that the practical results are similar." n78 They further say that,

> at the end of the [comparative] study, the same presumption acts as a means of checking our results: the comparatist can rest content if his researches through all the relevant material lead to the conclusion that the systems he has compared reach the same or... similar results, but if he finds that there are great differences or indeed diametrically opposite results, he should be put on notice to go back to check again... the terms in which he posed the original question.... n79

Thus, they view similarity among legal systems, not just as a likely result of comparative analysis, but as a confirmation of the validity of the comparative act. n80 The danger of such an approach, in my view, is that it is a tautology which may lead to a refusal to probe beneath the surface for underlying, sometimes irreconcilable, differences among legal systems. Even purely functionalist objectives, such as harmonizing international laws, drafting effective treaties, and understanding the resolutions to legal issues in other countries, will be undermined by the failure to consider incompatible features of different legal systems. To deny difference is to deny recognition to the particulars that constitute identify itself; in that sense, it is to camouflage and erase identity.

When understood in its own historical context, however, the similarity approach becomes more comprehensible, and perhaps may give pause to comparatists ready to rush headlong into a quest for differences in order to remedy the wrongs of past comparative legal analysis. The unspoken subtext to the Zweigert and Kötz similarity approach, and the one which has haunted comparative legal analysis in the United States for the past half century, is constituted by categorizations and associations the authors do not discuss or question, and of which they may not be fully aware, precisely because those associations are fundamental, unchallenged assumptions in their particular legal culture.

Zweigert and Kötz's scholarly writing post-dates the Second World War, and so has been done in the shadow of the holocaust, in a society anxious to disavow all traces of the Nuremberg laws' absolutist generalizations of people considered not merely different, but alien and subhuman. Their tendency to seek universals and obliterate differences among legal cultures in my view derives from the unstated assumption, pervasive in their legal culture since 1945, that where law recognizes and legitimizes difference, particularly as to fundamental human attributes, it will be for pernicious purposes of exclusion and discrimination. n81

Zweigert and Kötz, whose seminal work influenced comparative law both in Europe and the United States, were themselves greatly influenced by the comparatist scholars who fled Hitler's Europe, and most particularly Germany and Austria, during the Nazi period. Among the refugees were those who became the leading United States comparatists of the post-war era. The powerful influence the émigrés exerted on the study and teaching of comparative law in both the United States and Germany is the subject of a book recently published in Germany, which notes that fully one third of Germany's law professors emigrated after Hitler came to power n82

One who exerted a primordial influence on Zweigert and Kötz was Ernst Rabel, as the substantive thrust of their book reveals, and as their frequent quotes of Rabel and tributes to him make explicit. Rabel was a law professor who had enjoyed enormous prestige before Hitler came to power. In 1917, Rabel established the Munich Institute for Comparative Law, and in 1926 he became the head of the prestigious Kaiser Wilhelm Institute of Foreign and International Public Law. Rabel was also Germany's first representative to the International Institute for the Unification of Private Law, which the League of Nations founded in 1927, and which was the precursor to the Hague and Vienna Conventions that culminated in the U.N. Convention on Contracts for the International Sale of Goods. He also served as a judge of the Court of International Justice at the Hague and was President of the International Association of Comparative Law. n83

In 1939, after having been stripped of his professional positions, assets and civil rights, and formally forbidden to enter the premises of the institutes he had founded, he left Germany to start a new life in the United States at the age of 65. n84 He was made a Research Associate at the University of Michigan. n85 Rabel focused vehemently on the underlying similarity of peoples through the study of their legal systems. His focus in my opinion was marked by his personal experience, first as part of a people considered alien in Austria and Germany, and then by his exile from both home and native language.

Of the common and civil law systems, he wrote confidently and optimistically towards the end of his life that "they move steadily nearer to each other." n86 One also finds the following sentence in his Private Laws of Western Civilization: "The primordial steps leading us from isolation to community in the legal field, are in comparative research." n87 I would submit that these words held personal significance for Rabel. The great appeal of comparative law was to confirm belongingness and community even to one who had been abruptly and ruthlessly uprooted from his community. But if, as he wrote, community was to be found through comparative research, it could only be so if the results of that research underscored the profound similarity of humankind and human societies. n88

Rabel's objective of locating similarities was explicit, and was the motivating force behind his espousal of the functionalist approach to comparative legal analysis: "Practical solutions deserve the more intense interest, and a comparison of those solutions will be richly rewarded with regard to most legal issues. When viewed in this manner, the similarities will prove to be extraordinarily strong and thoroughly profound." n89

Rabel's influence on comparative law in the United States was not just through his personal presence here, but also through the influence he had had on many students in Germany who became fellow émigrés to the United States, n90 and were to teach comparative law to America's law students. Most of the émigrés who became important authorities on comparative law in the United States had been students of Rabel at one time, or students of others who taught at Rabel's institutes: people such as Max Rheinstein, Rudolf Schlesinger and Wolfgang Friedmann. n91 Many of the original editors of the American Journal of Comparative Law, founded in 1952, were also German émigrés, and the American Association for the Comparative Study of Law, which founded the Journal, was created as an American counterpart to Rabel's institutes. n92

These comparatist professors, who have been influential to this day in the study and teaching of comparative law in the United States (as well as in Germany) favored the assumption of a unified humanity. The logical consequence of this assumption was to focus on functionalism in comparative law, since functionalism operates at the most manifest level of society and allows a maximum of latitude for deëmphasizing the differences in legal mentality that frequently underlie practical resolutions to legal questions. Functionalism also tends to disguise the fact that a given question will itself mean some thing different in different legal cultures. n93

Like Rabel, Edgar Bodenheimer, also an émigré, believed that civilization depends on identifying universal human attributes and the legal principles suited to them. n94 Bodenheimer expressed the normative content of his theoretical stance unambiguously. Writing in 1940, Bodenheimer argued that "today, when law is in more than 'double jeopardy', we cannot afford the luxury of a positivistic jurisprudence." n95 Hitler's National Socialist régime frequently is an explicit point of reference in Bodenheimer's book, *Jurisprudence*, and is an implicit one throughout. n96 Like Rabel, Bodenheimer conceived of law's most pressing task as identifying the fundamental attributes that unify all of humankind by mirroring the natural laws which are deducible from those attributes, and which can ensure justice in all societies. From his premise of law as being "primarily a rational institution," Bodenheimer deemed attacks on reason to be attacks on the law, n97 and described as the "cult of irrationality" the view that law is a function of culture. n98

The émigrés' unspoken assumption was that the road to social and legal inclusion of diverse ethnic populations in any polity was by an insistence on fundamental sameness, with a concomitant trivialization or even denial of human diversity. They did not consider that the acknowledgment of diversity might be compatible with tolerance and inclusion. n105

The émigré comparatists intended the denial of difference to be the theoretical underpinning for the societal and legal tolerance of difference. The émigrés' personal experiences led to their faith in the fundamental similarity of all humans, and to their belief in the perniciousness of according legal recognition to differences in religious or ethnic origin. Their commitment to a theory of inclusion did not, however, extend to an inclusion of others' differentiating attributes, but to a levelling absorption, a homogeneity to be born of the erasure of difference rather than a homogeneity of common genetic back ground. It should be remembered that the émigré comparatists generally led highly assimilated lives. The Nazi classifications that had differentiated them from their German neighbors therefore would have seemed all the more absurd to them.

Some of the émigrés, like Rabel, who were of Jewish origin but professed the Christian faith, were not even separable on the basis of religious practice. Yet perceived differences based on heritage nevertheless suddenly condemned them under the Third Reich to an officially, legally sanctioned and mandated progressive dispossession of civil and material rights, and ultimately to subjugation, deportation, torture and death by mass extermination. It is not hard to surmise that such a state of affairs would have seemed no less than mad to the émigrés, as it did and does to many others. The paradox of their position, however, lies in that the logical consequence of an a priori denial of difference is not a tolerance of difference, but only tolerance of a sameness attempting to camouflage difference as sameness.

The émigrés' assumption that sameness is and must be synonymous with inclusion, and its converse that difference is synonymous with exclusion, leave minorities and others who are outside of the mainstream open to tragic consequences if ever their differences are acknowledged. Insistence on finding sameness may help to perpetuate the very human tragedies of exclusion that the émigrés dedicated themselves to eradicating from the future. The categorization of sameness with inclusion is not founded in logic, I believe, but in the happenstances of history, and in part on the profound effect that the trauma of Nazism and fascism exerted on the field of comparative law in the United States for over half a century, through the generation of the leaders in the field who were once targets of fascist persecution.

Antisemitic repression in the Nazi-dominated world had focused explicitly on "otherness" as a justification and legitimization of exclusion. The Nazi political philosopher Carl Schmitt defined the enemy as

> simply the Other, the Alien, and it is enough for his being that he is in a particularly intensive sense existentially something Other and Alien, so that in the case of conflict he means the negation of one's own form of existence and therefore must be guarded from and fought off, in order to pre serve one's own appropriate form of life. n107

As Richard Weisberg has noted with respect to the infamous Vichy trial of Léon Blum, a pre-war French Jewish prime minister, "the preliminary examination into the...charges against him...indicate that the 'making strange' of Léon Blum was at the heart of the matter." n108 Weisberg also reports that André Broc, a legal scholar, sought to generate support for the antisemitic racial laws of the period by arguing the "otherness" of Judaism: "[Although Broc's] citations to the Talmud and other Jewish texts and 'rules' are almost always erroneous or totally fabricated, the Talmud nonetheless symbolizes the ineffable 'otherness' that legitimizes—nay necessitates—the imposition of the status of 'other' through the law." n109

The word "foreigner" became interchangeable for "Jew". The pro-fascist *Action française* party pledged its members to oppose France's pre-war government on the ground that "the Republic of France is the reign of the foreigner." n110 In Germany,

Nazi propaganda against the pre-war French government also equated the French Republic with the otherness of Jews, with Julius Streicher going so far as to describe the French revolutionary slogan *liberté, égalité, fraternité* as "a slogan from the Talmud's kitchen." n111

Consistently with their theory of human universality, the émigrés implicitly treated the Nazi creed to persecute the other as a universal and inalterable human trait, rather than as an aberration or historically contingent phenomenon. It is useful in this context to bear in mind, however, that until the nineteenth century no theory identified nations with common genetic ascendancy or a common language. n112 This fact greatly reduces the persuasiveness of the émigrés' conviction of the inseparability of difference from persecution.

At the time of the French Revolution, for example, fifty percent of the French population could not speak French at all and only twelve to thirteen percent spoke it correctly. Similarly, only two and a half percent of Italy's population spoke Italian in 1860 when the country was unified. n113 Moreover, in sixteenth-century England, the English word for "foreigner" still referred to those who lived in a neighboring county, and English people generally did not speak the same language as those in different counties. The fact that the concept of nationhood has been coupled with the idea of a homogeneous population only in recent times undermines the assumption that a diverse population must first be represented and understood as non-diverse in order for minorities to be secure. n115

The émigré comparatists' faith in natural law, in inviolable, universally applicable principles of law, was a movement in counterdirection to the progression which German jurisprudence had been taking after Kant, away from naturalism.n116 The disjunctive note that the émigrés created in German legal theory signals a point of rupture occurring beneath the surface level. I believe that it was born of a lifetime of being considered outsiders, albeit at first assimilated outsiders, culminating in the trauma of Nazi persecution. The émigrés' conviction that objective theory and natural laws should be the basis for legal analysis took the form of a rejection of realism, but paradoxically was itself in large measure caused by their reaction to the devastating power over law of the social and political realities of Nazi Europe. The émigrés' conclusions were influenced by antisemitism, and later also totalitarianism, both of which militated against the émigrés' acceptance of a realist approach to law. They were persuaded that social, political and legal reality was so catastrophic as a basis for law and legal theory that evidence supporting the validity of legal realism had to be denied and combatted. n117

The Third Reich posed particular problems to the legal theorist in that it wore the mantle of a highly legalistic society. n118 Statutes and decrees legalized terror and racism. Unlike many other dictatorships, the Nazi régime was lawless principally in the sense that it was characterized by the enactment of what might be called anti-laws, rather than by breaches of enacted law. n119 One might also say that the régime mimicked law, and that this mimicry was more threatening than an absence of law, because it challenged legal theory's ability to expose and identify the fraud perpetrated by German legal rhetoric.

The legal scholars who fled Nazi Germany fled a system of laws characterized in their eyes by the cruel absurdity of the law's denial of universal human sameness. Their fervent belief in the need to see all people as fundamentally alike was part of an ideology of, on the one hand, inclusion based on commonality, and, on the other hand, law as an objective, scientific field, capable of debunking and discrediting the measures that had passed for law and generally had been accepted as such in Nazi Germany and occupied Europe. n120

NOTES

n76. Konrad Zweigert & Hein Kötz, An Introduction to Comparative Law 39 (in two volumes; Tony Weir, trans. 1977). The functionalist approach, developed by Ernst Rabel, has been the hallmark of contemporary comparative legal analysis. See Mary Ann Glendon, et al., Comparative Legal Traditions 11 (1994) (describing functionalism as "comparative law's principal gift to 20th century legal science"). The focus on functionalism is suited to yielding results of similiarity because it does not stray from the surface level of functional results to legal problems to societal, historical, and cultural underpinnings. Those underpinnings, however, are embedded in the results, and ignored at the risk of significant misapprehension. Rabel believed that "international collaboration" would "correct" misperceptions stemming from a comparatist's ignorance of the target culture's differences. 16 RabelsZeitschrift, at 359 (1951). One has only to study the various and varying interpretations of treaties such as the U.N. Convention on Contracts for the International Sale of Goods (the treaty which eventually emerged from the successor to the Hague Convention which Rabel had attended as Germany's representative) to wonder whether uniformity or a Tower of Babel is the more logical outcome of international collaboration, even where uniformity of interpretation is a stated goal. See Harry Flechtner, "Sources of Textual Nonuniformity in the U.N. Sales Convention: The Several CISGs, Address to the Third International Workshop on a Legal Expert System for the U.N. Convention on contracts for the International Sale of Goods" (1995); Farnsworth, "A Common Lawyer's View of His Civilian Colleagues," 57 La. L. Rev. 227 (1996); and Curran, "The Interpretive Challenge to Uniformity," 15 J.L. & Comm. 175, 175–79 (1995).

n77. Id. at 31.

n78. Id.

n79. Id. at 31. Accord, Burt, "Judges, Behavioral Scientists, and the Demands of Humanity," 143 U. Pa. L. Rev. 179 (1994) ("Unless judges and scientists alike em phasize our human commonalities — unless they emphasize the underlying social and psychological forces that can promise to draw us together — then we will be fated to drive one another further and further apart.") See also id., at 184–85 ("If human beings focused clearly and rationally on the descriptive scientific proposition that we are all fundamentally alike in our nature, then we would be more inclined to view one another with sympathy, with mutual understanding and fellow feeling.")

n80. Zweigert and Kötz's presumption of similarity echoes a similar methodological approach by Savigny, who concluded that any observed legal material should be dis missed as irrelevant if it clashed with the presumption that German law was an organic whole. See Reimann, supra n. 42, at 885–87. It should be noted that Zweigert and Kötz suggest that the presumption of similarity is not a universally valid method of approaching comparative analysis, and that there are areas influenced by history, religion and culture with respect to which the comparatist cannot assume similarity. These areas, however, in their view are restricted, and "mainly to be found in family law and the law of succession." Zweigert & Kötz, supra, n. 76, at 31.

n81. While post-war German legal culture reflected a reaction against Nazism, it was not free of the influence of formerly active members of the Nazi judicial system. The noted constitutional law scholar Theodor Maunz, for instance, active under the Nazis and a former student of Nazi legal philosopher Carl Schmitt, reportedly was a supporter of extremist right-wing groups until his death in1993. See Michael Stolleis, Juristen: Ein biographisches Lexikon 416 (1995). For the post-war pro-Nazi leanings of the German judiciary, see Ingo Müller, Hitler's Justice: The Courts of the Third Reich 219–98 (Deborah Lucas Schneider trans., 1991). For the continued post-war presence in German law faculties of law professors who actively supported the Nazi regime, see id.; and Reimann, "National Socialist Jurisprudence and Academic Con tinuity: A Comment on Professor Kaufmann's Article," 9 Cardozo L. Rev. 1651 (1988).

n82. Kinkel, "Eröffnungsansprache," in Der Einfluß der Deutschen Emigranten auf die Rechtsentwicklung in den USA und Deutschland at 3–8 (Marcus Lutter et al., ed., 1993) (hereinafter Der Einfluß). For a Nazi complaint about the profound degree of Jewish influence on Germany's law faculties, see Schmitt, "Die deutsche Rechtswissenschaft in Kampf gegen den jüdischen Geist," 41 Deutsche Juristen-Zeitung (1936). See also Langbein, supra n. 31, at 547 (describing comparative law in the United States as "[a]" refugee field... [with] Rheinstein at Chicago, Schlesinger at Cornell, Ehrenzweig and Reisenfeld at Berkeley, Kessler (and now Damaska) at Yale, Rabel and Stein at Michigan.")

n83. I list here only a portion of his pre-war positions. For a more complete enumeration, see the forewords to Rabel's The Conflict of Laws[:] A Comparative Study (1958) by William Draper Lewis, at ix–xiii; and by Hessel E.Yntema, at xiii–xxi. For two excellent portrayals of Rabel's professional contributions after emigration, see Clark, "The Influence of Ernst Rabel on American Law" in Der Einfluß, at 107–26; and Großfeld & Winship, "Der Rechtsgelehrte in der Fremde," at 189–200, in Der Einfluß.

n84. For a discussion of the letters sent by the rectors of German universities to "non-Aryan" professors, to forbid them access to their universities, see Hannah Ar endt's correspondence with Karl Jaspers, "Hannah Arendt to Karl Jaspers, July 9, 1946," in Hannah Arendt/Karl Jaspers Correspondence 1926–1969 (Lotte Kohler & Hans Saner eds.; Robert Kimer & Rita Kimber trans). For Heidegger's ignominious behavior as rector towards Husserl, to whom Heidegger owed his position, see id. and Elizbieta Ettinger, Hannah Arendt/Martin Heidegger 96–97 (1995). For a detailed account in diary form of the increasingly constricted and beleaguered life in Germany of a professor whose situation parallelled that of Rabel (i.e., a professor of the Christian faith, but of Jewish ancestry, married to an "Aryan"), including the almost daily progression of his professional humiliation and demise, see Victor Klemperer, Ich will Zeugnis Ablegen bis zum Letzten: Tagebücher 1933–1941; 1942–1945 (1996, in two volumes; English translation scheduled to appear in 1998); see also Ruth Lewin Sine, Lise Meitner: A Life in Physics (1996) (Biography of a "non-Aryan" woman physicist who, like Rabel, had been born in   Austria and was therefore protected from the antisemitic laws until the *Anschluß*, and thereafter fled to Sweden and Denmark with the assistance of Niels Bohr.)

n85. For a poignant account of Rabel's life as a research associate at the University of Michigan, including a post-war confession by Michigan Law School's dean that the faculty had no idea of Rabel's former eminence, see "Wir wußten nicht, wer er war," in Winship & Großfeld's beautiful tribute to Rabel, Der Einfluß, supra n. 83, at 189–90.

n86. Rabel, "Private Laws of Western Civilization," 10 La. L. Rev. 431, 432 (1950).

n87. Id. at 460 (emphasis added). David Clark also notes this sentence of Rabel's as significant in his essay on Rabel in Der Einfluß, supra n. 82, at 117.

n88. One wonders if similar personal motives might underlie the genesis of Levi-Straussian structural anthropolgy. Levi-Strauss' life story shared much with Rabel's in terms of assimilation and exile, and his research, like Rabel's, focused on societal differences as a way of discovering and uncovering fundamental structures inherent in all human societies. The late Rudolf Schlesinger, another highly influential émigré comparatist, developed a "common core" approach in keeping with Rabel's outlook.

n89. Ernst Rabel, 1 Das Recht des Warenkaufs: Eine rechtsvergleichende Darstellung 67 (1964, originally published 1936–58) (trans. and cited in Hyland, "Comparative Law," in A Companion to the Philosophy of Law and Legal Theory 187 (Dennis Patterson, ed. 1996) (emphasis added).

n90. One of those former students, Max Rheinstein, a former *Assistent* of Rabel's in Germany, was also to be instrumental in enabling Rabel to escape from Germany in 1939, a date when emigration to the United States was already becoming perilously difficult.

n91. For a more thorough list of the many émigré comparative law professors whom Rabel greatly influenced, see Clark, "The Influence of Ernst Rabel on American Law," in Der Einfluß, supra n. 82, at 107–26. Of Rabel's pervasive, continuing influence on comparatists in the United States to date, David Gerber writes that the "methodology initially developed by Ernst Rabel at the Kaiser Wilhelm Institute in Berlin in the 1920s [is] the current state-of-the-art methodology, at least in Northern Europe and the United States." Paper delivered at conference on new directions in comparative law, Hastings Law School, September, 1997, on file with the author.

n92. See Clark, id.

n93. For an example of an apparently identical legal question which masks fundamental underlying differences in different legal systems, one might posit two nations working on replacing welfare payments to single parents with obligatory, government-created jobs. If each nation enacted the same provision on its face, the law nevertheless would be very different in significance if in one country the government also provided free day care for children, while in the other no provisions were made for child care and day care centers were nonexistent because the second country viewed childrearing as the exclusive responsibility of mothers.

n94. See Durham, Jr., "Edgar Bodenheimer: Conservator of Civilized Legal Culture," in Der Einfluß, at 127, esp. the section entitled The Defense of Natural Law, at 136–40. Professor Clark also notes Rabel's overweening goal of, in Rabel's own words, "healing the great schism in the western legal world and...uniting its juristic effort and accomplishments." Id. at 114.

n95. Edgar Bodenheimer, Jurisprudence vii (1940) (emphasis added). It should be noted that the connection between positivism and Nazism has been, and continues to be, the subject of interest and debate. See e.g., Hart, "Positivism and the Separation of Law and Morals," 71 Harv. L. Rev. 593 (1958); Fuller, supra n. 5; Müller, supra n. 81; Osiel, "Dialogue with Dictators," 20 L. & Soc. Inquiry 481 (1995); Richard L. Weisberg, Vichy Law and the Holocaust in France 390–402, and sources cited therein, esp. at 394, n. 12 (1996); and Judith Shklar, Legalism: Laws, Morals and Political Trials (1964). The debate was launched with the post-war rejection of positivism by the formerly positivistic German legal philosopher, Gustav Radbruch. See Ott & Buob, "Did Legal Positivists Render

German Jurists Defenceless during the Third Reich?," 2 Soc. & Legal Studies 91 (1993).

n96. Bodenheimer's effort seems in keeping with Carl Schmitt's characterization of the liberal rule of law as repressing the political in Carl Schmitt, Verfassungslehre 41 (1965) (1928), although the effort to depoliticize law of course is itself a political act. Cf. also Carl Schmitt's definition of the political as the possibility of distinguishing friend from foe. Id. at 169.

n97. Bodenheimer, supra n. 95, at vii.

n98. Edgar Bodenheimer, Philosophy as Responsibility 222 (1980). Cf. Yntema, "Comparative Legal Research: Some Remarks on 'Looking Out of the Cave'," 54 Mich. L. Rev. 899, 903 (1956) ("comparative law has a universal humanistic outlook... like other branches of science, it contemplates that... the problems of justice are basically the same in time and space throughout the world"); and Rheinstein, "Teaching Tools in Comparative Law," 1 Am. J. Comp. L. 95, 98 (19) ("Comparative law... is the observational and exactitude-seeking science of law in general. Its subject matter is constituted by the laws of all times and all climes.")

---

n105. The émigrés' interpretation of Goethe conforms to the views expressed in re cent books by two French authors, the philosopher Alain Finkielkraut and the semiotician Julia Kristeva. See Alain Finkielkraut, La Défaite de la Pensée (1995); and Julia Kristeva, Nations Without Nationalism (Leon Roudiez, trans., 1993). These authors contrast Goethe and Montesquieu to Herder, exalting the former as representatives of the Enlightenment's focus on universality and tolerance, and criticizing the latter as a precursor of Hitler. The Goethe/Herder debate is beyond the scope of this article, but it has significant implications for comparative legal analysis, and is the subject of a separate article, Curran, " Herder and the Holocaust: A Debate About Difference and Determinism in the Context of Comparative Law," in The Holocaust's Ghost: Writings on Art, Politics, Law and Education (ed.s,F.C. DeCoste & Bernard Schwartz (2000).

n107. Schmitt, "Der Begriff des Philosophischen," in Carl Schmitt, Leo Strauss und "der Begriff des Politischen": Dialog unter Abwesenden 4 (H. Meir ed., 1988; trans. Scheuerman, in "Modernist Antimodernist: Carl Schmitt's Concept of the Political," 19 Phil. & Social Criticism 79, 84 (1993).

n108. See Blum, "The 'Stranger' at Riom: Legalized Ostracism and Vichy's Political Trial," in Richard Weisberg, Vichy Law and the Holocaust in France 28 (1996).

n109. Id., at 27.

n110. "France," in Alistair Hamilton, The Appeal of Fascism: A Study of Intellectuals and Fascism 1919–1945 (1971), quoted in Hartman, "Is an Aesthetic Ethos Possible? Night Thoughts After Auschwitz," 5 Cardozo Studies L. & Lit. 135, 144 (1995).

n111. Das Dritte Reich und die Juden 20 (Léon Poliakov & Joseph Wulf eds., 1989), quoted in Hartman, id., at 144.

n112. See Robert Hobsbawm, Nations and Nationalism Since 1780: Programme, Myth, Reality 104 (1990). For an analysis of the eighteenth-century roots of nineteenth-century nationalism, see "On the Rise of Nationalism," in Isaiah Berlin, The Crooked Timber of Humanity: Chapters in the History of Ideas 238–61 (1992).

n113. Hobsbawm, supra n. 112, at 60–61.

n114. See Marianne Constable, The Law of the Other: The Mixed Jury and Changing Conceptions of Citizenship, Law, and Knowledge, esp. 112–27 (1995); Hobsbawm, supra n. 112, at 54, for the view that national languages are often artificial constructs foisted on people to shape them into a nation. Far from being the foundations of national cultures, national languages historically have been "attempts to devise a standardized idiom out of a multiplicity of actually spoken idioms, which are thereafter downgraded to dialects." See also Nietzsche, "First Essay," reprinted in On the Gene alogy of Morals and Ecce Homo, 2, 25–26 (Walter Kauffmann ed., 1989) ("the origin of language itself [is] an expression of power on the part of the rulers..."), quoted in Winter, "The Power Thing," 82 Va. L. Rev. 721, 735, n. 49. But see Kristeva, supra n. 105, at 18 (the origin of the word "barbarous" is "the incomprehensible language of those who do not share the Greeks' mother tongue.")

n115. See Hobsbawm, supra n. 112, at 21–22 (Nationhood and homogeneous populations need not be inextricably connected, and the concept of nation is a recent historical phenomenon, rather than an unchanging entity. Moreover, substantial differences in the concept exist in different countries.); and de Witte, "Droits fondamentaux et protection de la diversité linguistique," in Language and Law: Proceedings of the First Conference of the International Institute of Comparative Linguistic Law 97 (P. Pupier et al., eds., 1988) (evoking Aristotelian concept that uniform treat ment of different people results in inequality). See also Emmanuel Levinas, Time and the Other 83 (Richard A. Cohen, trans. 1987) ("alterity appears as a nonreciprocal relationship...the Other as Other is not only an alter ego: the Other is what I myself am not. The Other is this, not because of the Other's character, or physiognomy or psychology, but because of the Other's very alterity.") But, for Levinas, otherness need not imply negativity. Richard Cohen writes of Levinas that "to grasp alterity outside even negativity, and thus in a truly positive "sense," is perhaps the essence of Levinas' entire work." Id. at 83, n. 63.

n116. For a history of German jurisprudence, see Reimann, supra n. 42. See Osiel, "Dialogue With Dictators: Judicial Resistance in Argentina and Brazil," 20 L. & Soc. Inquiry 481, 502 (1995) for naturalism's appeal as a guarantor of judicial resistance to unjust laws. ("Advocates of [naturalism] have claimed that naturalism facilitates resistance to unjust law by requiring judges to inspect official decrees and enactments for their morality before classifying the demands they impose as legally binding.") See also David, "Existe-t-il un droit occidental," in Xxth Century Comparative and Conflicts Law 56, 64 (Kurt H. Nadelmann et al., eds., 1961)

("*La renaissance de l'idée de Droit naturel, après la deuxième guerre mondiale, a d'autre part créé un climat nouveau. L'unité du monde occidental enfin est apparue à beaucoup comme une necessité, à la réalisation de laquelle devaient contribuer les juristes, en face de la menace que représentaient, pour l'idéal auquel ils sont attachés, tels ou tels autres régimes politiques.*") Ingo Müller suggests a more sinister reason for the espousal of natural law and rejection of positivism by some post-war German judges. According to Müller, post-war judges who had sat on the bench during Hitler's time tried to whitewash their formerly zealously Nazi decisions by falsely claiming after 1945 to have been legal positivists who merely had followed the letter of the law, and therefore were personally blameless for their past decisions. Even worse, by asserting the need to reject positivism in favor of naturalism, those judges were also erecting a theoretical basis of support for a future fight against reforms that the new democratic government might have in mind. See Müller, supra n. 81, at 223.

n117. But see Leibholz, "Constitutional Law and Constitutional Reality," in Festschrift für Karl Löwenstein 305, 308 (Henry Steele

Commager et al., eds., 1971) ("It must be the task of the constitutional lawyer to reconcile rules of law and constitutional reality in such a way that the existing dialectical conflict between rule and reality can be removed as far as possible by creative interpretation of the constitution without doing violence thereby either with reality in favour of the rule, or to the rule in favour of reality.") Leibholz emigrated to London, but wrote the above after his return to Germany, and with the experience of an acting judge. After the war, he was made a Justice of Germany's Federal Constitutional Court. Leibholz was the "non-Aryan" husband of the twin sister of Dietrich Bonhoeffer, the anti-Nazi German Confessional Church minister martyred in the wake of the failed July 1944 attempt against Hitler's life. For an account of Leibholz's years as an émigré, see Sabine Leibholz-Bonhoeffer, The Bonhoeffers: Portrait of a Family (1971).

n118. See Raul Hilberg, The Politics of Memory: The Journey of a Holocaust Historian 77–80 (1996); Müller, supra n. 81; and Richard Lawrence Miller, Nazi Justiz: Law of the Holocaust (1995); and Steiner, supra n. 10, at 146.

n119. This caused difficulty in the international community of various kinds. See Lauterpacht, "The Nationality of Denationalized Persons," Jewish Y.B. Int'l L. 164 (1949); and Mann, "The Present Validity of Nazi Nationality Laws," 89 L.Q. Rev. 194 (1973). I owe my discovery of both of these fascinating studies to J.H.H. Weiler's excellent recent article, "Does Europe Need a Constitution? Reflections on Demos, Telos and the German Maastricht Decision," 1 Eur. L.J. 219 (1995).

(b) Questions

1. How does functionalism correlate with universalist tendencies in comparative law?

2. How has the concept of "otherness" evolved in the United States in the past century?

3. Have the concepts of nationality and nationhood evolved considerably in recent times? Do you think that nation-states may be a transitory phenomenon?

4. In what ways was the universalism of comparative legal analysis an intellectual countercurrent

    (a) from its inception?
    (b) from late twentieth-century views?

3. *An Example*

(a) Vivian Grosswald Curran, *Cultural Immersion*
46 American Journal of Comparative Law pp. 78–83

The *Volkswagen* Case

We have seen above how historical events contributed to the categorization of difference with exclusion, and that this underlying association has affected the conduct of comparative legal analysis in the United States. A multitude of other categorizations affect and define our legal culture. In this section, I try to illustrate the challenges of cultural immersion through a critique of John Dawson's commentary on a German court opinion. I hope to illuminate how analysis suffers when the comparatist does not take entrenched categorizations into consideration. I engage in this critique because I consider John Dawson to have been one of the most eminent and effective American legal comparatists. A scholar of rare erudition, Dawson steeped him self in original documents from past centuries, and studied them with a meticulousness and thoroughness that allowed him to uncover in numerable unchallenged interpretive mistakes. n121 That even a scholar of such skill and erudition should "misread" is, in my opinion, illustrative of the degree to which underlying cultural phenomena, often considered extrinsic to law, influence legal analysis and the conception of law.

In an article on judicial revisions of frustrated contracts, Dawson recounted a German decision he found illogical, baffling and unjustified. n122 The *Volkswagen* case was decided by the *Bundesgerichtshof* in 1951. n123 It involved a contract entered into by Volkswagen in the late 1930's. The plaintiffs were two buyers who had ordered and made prepayments on Volkswagen cars in 1938 and 1939. Over 300,000 other Germans had also made prepayments on pre-war orders from Volkswagen in a project endorsed by Hitler, allegedly to enable the German *Volk* to purchase affordable cars. The totality of the pre-war car payments involved in this government-sponsored project amounted to over 250,000,000 marks. They were in a bank account in Berlin, with the account title in the name of the official Nazi organization which ran the Volkswagen project.

Before the cars were manufactured, however, war broke out, and the government appropriated the defendant's factory for war production. At the end of the war, the Russian occupying force in Berlin took the bank account containing the car prepayment funds.

When Volkswagen resumed manufacturing cars after the war, the plaintiffs sued for their cars, asking the court to fix an appropriate price, and conceding that to require a car for the original price would be grossly unfair to the manufacturer. The case eventually reached the *Bundesgerichtshof*, which held the pre-war contracts to be enforceable.

Dawson reacted with both disagreement and amused amazement to this decision which entailed, for reasons that need not be discussed here, the lower court's tracking down thousands of persons situated similarly to the plaintiffs. The court would have to conduct a detailed factfinding that would be burdensome in the extreme, if not impossible, due to the massive nature of German war casualties and the large-scale territorial displacements which had followed the war. Dawson wrote with some humor that "the trial judge to whom the case was returned [for the fact-finding referred to above] must have had the sensation that he was wandering lonely as a cloud among the daffodils as he sat about performing these multifarious tasks." n124 Dawson was particularly baffled by the fact that a decision he considered absurdly wrong-headed was not hotly criticized by respected German legal authorities: "Criticism in Germany of this astonishing case was extremely mild." n125.

To Dawson, the Court clearly was in error. As he saw it, under German contract law, the contract's foundations had been destroyed by the catastrophic events of the war, such that performance was no longer feasible, and, therefore, the Court should have rescinded the contracts pursuant to the BGB's *Wegfall der Geschäftsgrundlage* provision. n126 Dawson believed that the non-feasibility was in part a function of the overwhelming burden on the court that would result from a judicial revision of the contracts. He reached this conclusion through a common-law perspective, however. The German standard for enforcing contracts did not look to judicial burden. As Dawson himself reported, the German standard required a contract to be enforced if feasible, and contracts were deemed feasible if at least a rough approximation of the original promise still could be performed. n127 As the German court saw it, since the defendant still manufactured cars, the defendant could still perform at least an approximation of its original promise, albeit with a different kind of car, and at a price to be determined by the Court.

Significantly, Dawson reproduced the sentence from the *Bundesgerichtshof's* decision which in my opinion contains the clue to its holding, but found it neither significant nor illuminating: The Court set forth the principle that "in law it is a basic premise that contracts should be performed." n128 Dawson dismissed this statement as beside the point: "Wholly laudable though this proposition might... be, there would remain one other question—whether it had any thing whatever to do with this case." n129

It had everything to do with the case, and everything to do with the difference between the common and civil law perspectives of contract law. The binding nature of a promise is of utmost importance to the civil law, and the courts accordingly bind individuals to their promises. n130 The *Bürgerliches Gesetzbuch*, Germany's Civil Code, sets forth explicitly in Section 241 that, "the effect of an obligation is that the creditor is entitled to claim performance..." n131 As Professors Flour and Aubert write in their appropriately titled book on the French law of contracts, *Obligations*, morality dominates civilian contract law. n132 They state unequivocally that "the legal obligation incumbent on the contracting party to perform is none other than the moral duty to honor one's word, once given." n133 The civilian focus on morality contrasts with the common law's concern for efficiency as the primary priority. The contrast between the two systems is not only pervasive but fundamental, influencing the courts' assessments of factual criteria.

The evolution of morality as the dominant focus of civilian contract law has a long history in continental Europe. Canon law made morality the guiding principle of contract law, upholding promises even if deficient in form: "In all cases a promise is to be performed, even if naked according to the canons...because God does not distinguish between simple words and an oath." n134 Flour and Aubert signal the evolution from Roman formalism to consensualism as Christianity's innovation and contribution. n135 The law had formally adopted morality as its standard for contract analysis in thirteenth-century France, and by the sixteenth century in Freiburg. n136

In the seventeenth century, Pufendorf transformed the ecclesiastical idea of natural law into a secular vision, and articulated the maxim *pacta sunt servanda* ("commitments must be honored"), which was to have a decisive influence on international treaty law.n137 Pufendorf, like the canonists, believed in natural law. Pufendorf, unlike Hobbes, but like Grotius before him and Montesquieu after him, believed that humans are naturally sociable and that peace is a natural state, but, like Hobbes, Pufendorf evaluated states of peace as fragile and precarious. n138

This moral conception was translated into the civil codes of Europe by making specific performance the normal remedy for breach of contract, and monetary damages the exception, in contradistinction to the common law system of monetary remedies as the norm and specific performance the exception. Similarly, the common law's stark delineation between tort and contract law is alien to the civil law, with the concept of "fault" indispensable to civil law contract analysis, while unfamiliar in common law contract analysis. n139

To a common-law lawyer trained in the Holmesian tradition, the *Volkswagen* case offers a prime example of a breach far more efficient than performance would be, and which therefore should have been judicially sanctioned. To the civilian court, however, the many and serious practical difficulties involved in the judicial enforcement of performance were outweighed by the fact that a commitment had been made to a buyer who had paid in acceptance of the commitment. n140 The *Volkswagen* decision makes sense if one recognizes the extent to which morality informs the civilian law of contracts, and, consequently, that judicial enforcement of promises is a tenet central to the civilian vision of the nature of contracts. Familiarity with the text of German law does not enable one to assess the primacy morality plays in the civil law's concept of contracts. The emphasis or degree of weight a court accords to various considerations often are determinative of the case's outcome, and often emanate from traditions rooted in a nation's historical, political, economic and social development.

NOTES

n121. See, e.g., John P. Dawson, The Oracles of the Law (1968); and Dawson, "Specific Performance in France and Germany," 57 Mich. L. Rev. 495 (1959).

n122. Dawson, "Judicial Revision of Frustrated Contracts," 63 B.U.L. Rev. 1039, 1083–88 (1983).

n123. 61 BGHZ 31 (1973).

n124. Id. at 1085.

n125. Id. at 1086.

n126. This provision concerns such fundamental change in conditions that the foundations for the contract no longer make sense. It is to be distinguished from (1) *Unmöglichkeit*, where the contract's unique features render it unperformable by another; (2) *Unvermögen*, where, objectively speaking, the contract could be performed by another promisor; and (3) positive *Vertragsverletzung*, where the promisee suffers affirmative injury from the promisor.

n127. Id.

n128. Id. at 1086.

n129. Id.

n130. See René David, Les Contrats en droit anglais at para. 101 (2d ed., 1985). See also Richard Hyland's beautiful and erudite analysis in "Pacta Sunt Servanda: A Meditation," 34 Va. J. Int L. 405 (1994). (Morality characterizes civilian contract law); and Barry Nicolas, The French Law of Contracts 39 (1992) (Characterizing civil law contract analysis in terms of agreement, in contrast to the common law's focus on consideration). See also id. at 41; and 241(Validity of unilateral contracts in France, such as promise to make a loan; and requirement that creditor apply to the court for an order rescinding the contract where debtor has breached, in contrast to common law creditor's right to treat debtor's breach as discharging the contract); Norbert Horn et al., German Private and Commercial Law: An Introduction 141 (1982) (importance of *pacta sunt servanda* to German concept of contract); and Mattei, "The Comparative Law and Economics of Penalty Clauses in Contracts," 43 Am. J. Comp. L. 427, 441 (1995) (contrasting the significant difference between the civil and common law systems' "impact on the promisor's decision to breach or not to breach").

n131. *"Kraft des Schuldverhältnisses ist der Gläubiger berechtigt, von dem Schuldner einem Leistung zu fordern."* (English translation from Simon L. Goren, The German Civil Code 41 (1994).

n132. *"Que le droit des obligations soit ainsi dominé par la morale, nul ne l'a jamais nié."* Jacques Flour & Jean-Luc Aubert, 1 Les Obligations 47 (1988).

n133. *"L'obligation juridique qui pèse sur tout débiteur contractuel, d'exécuter le contrat, n'est autre que le devoir moral de respecter la parole donnée."* Id. at 46 (emphasis in original). See also Powers, Jr., "Good and Bad Faith in Contract Law," 72 Tex. L. Rev. 1209, 1278 (1994) (analyzing U.S. contract law theory of efficient breach); and Poole, "Damages for Breach of Contract," 59 Modern L. Rev. 272, 272 (1996) ("In French law a distinction is drawn between the effects of intentional and unintentional breach…This is not, however, a factor in English decisions which do not distinguish breaches on an intent basis. Such an approach would also sit uneasily with the principle that contract damages do not seek to punish the guilty party.…")

n134. Hostensius, Summa Aurea, I, De Pactis 6 (1570), quoted in and translated by Richard Hyland, supra n. 130, at 417 (1994). See also Herman, "Utilitas Ecclesiae: The Canonical Conception of the Trust," 70 Tulane L. Rev. 2239 (1996).

n135. Flour & Aubert, supra n. 132, at 47. In Roman law, consensus was just one of four bases for a contract. See R. W. Leage, Roman Private Law Founded on the "Institutes" of Gaius and Justinian 264 (1909).

n136. See Hyland, supra n. 130, at 425, quoting in old French the French medieval rule that "*Convenance loi vaint*".

n137. See id. at 422; and Will, "Right to Require Performance," in Commentary on the International Sales Law: The 1980 Vienna Sales Convention 333–336 (Bianca & Bonnell, eds. 1987) (modern relevance to European contract law of pacta sunt servanda.)

n138. See Samuel Pufendorf, On the Duty of Man and Citizen (James Tully; ed. Michael Silverthorne, trans., 1991); Samuel Pufendorf, "Man Has Been Destined by Nature to Live a Social Life with Man," 3 Observations, in The Political Writings of Samuel Pufendorf 80–82 (Craig L. Carr; ed. Michael J. Seidler trans., 1994); and Hyland, supra n. 130, at 128. Pufendorf himself had suffered the effects of that precari ousness. Shortly after going to Denmark in 1658 to be a tutor to the children of the Swedish minister to Denmark, war broke out between Sweden and Denmark and Pufendorf was imprisoned. See Tully, supra this note. For an analysis of philosophies informed by fear, see Shklar, "The Liberalism of Fear," in Liberalism and the Moral Life 21–38 (Nancy L. Rosenblum ed., 1989). Neither Hobbes nor Pufendorf, both absolute monarchists, meet Shklar's criteria for liberalism, but her remarks on the formative influence of fear are highly apposite to both. Hyland offers an explanation for Pufendorf's fear intermingling with his optimism in that Pufendorf was writing on the heels of the Thirty Years' War. See Hyland, supra n. 130, at 423.

n139. For an overview of the paramount role of "fault" in French contract law, see "l'Analyse générale de la faute," in Jacques Flour & Jean-Luc Aubert, II Les Obligations 89–123 (1989). See also Legrand, "Judicial Revision of Contracts in French Law: A Case-Study," 62 Tul. L. Rev. 963 (1988) on the extent to which French courts revise contracts in order to promote morality and the sanctity of the promise. It is to be noted in particular that this judicial contract revision occurs despite France's general prohibition against judicial activism.

n140. See Farnsworth, "A Common Lawyer's View of His Civilian Colleagues," 57 La. L. Rev. 227, 235 (1996) (As United States representative at UNCITRAL, the United Nations Commission on International Trade Law, in negotiating and drafting what was to become the United Nations Convention on Contracts for the International Sale of Goods, Professor Farnsworth noted that the common law concept of efficient breach not only did "not travel well, but ... struck most of my civilian colleagues as bordering on the immoral.")

(b) Questions

1. In what different and even contradictory ways might a court apply a principle of "feasibility" to contract law?

2. Does the contrast between an ethics-based and an efficiency-based contract law correspond to other contrasts between the societies of Continental Europe and the United States?

3. What do you think the mjor obstacles might be for those who undertake comparative legal analysis?

III. Comparative Law as Translation

1. *Introduction*

The passages below expound and develop the concept that comparative legal analysis has much in common with translation, and that a close look at the processes involved in translation illuminates the comparative act that animates comparative law, as it does cognition itself.

2. *Intercultural Understanding*

(a). Bernhard Großfeld, Kernfragen der Rechtsvergleichung
(Mohr [Paul Siebeck])1996),
pp.118–122; pp. 106–115.1

Translation

Even where we are able to restrict ourselves to a foreign language, we encounter the same hindrances I have described with respect to our own language. They are still greater abroad, because each language expresses a concept with different emotional connotation, thus giving it another content. For example, the word "*selbstbewußt,*" literally translated, means "self-conscious" in English,

---

1. Translated by Vivian Grosswald Curran, footnotes omitted.

which in turn, however, signifies "shyness" [in contrast to its meaning in German]...

There are no intercultural synonyms. It is "utopian to believe that two words that belong to two different languages have exactly the same meaning."

A word, a sentence, a text are understandable first from the whole; that always is possible only to a limited extent. There are no identical trains of thought in two languages.

The chances of a translator often are held to be poor:

> In reality, the real world establishes itself largely unconsciously through the language customs of the group. No two languages exist that approximate each other closely enough to represent the same social reality. The worlds in which different societies live are different worlds, not even one and the same world with differing labels.

The barrier to intercultural understanding is particularly steep in law: "Several languages are not as many designations of one thing; they are different views of the same..."

Above all, for the intellectual, language *shapes* things. For law, moreover, the cast, the *precise* form, is decisive, the "how" one tells the "joke"! Accordingly, Koschaker asked "if with receptions in the field of law, the central point does not lie more in the form, and indeed as much in the external as in the form of thought, rather than in the content."

In comparative law, we cannot restrict ourselves to the literal translation of texts; for we want more than textual knowledge; we want effective, practical knowledge of the conceptual horizon. With literary texts, the translator is supposed to translate language rather than culture: "The translation of culture may leave the sons of the desert riding on horses instead of camels, in the village instead of the oasis, with church towers instead of minarets."

Comparative law, by contrast, requires an exchange of images. We must allow the concepts of the foreign law to become images and then describe them in our language....

Yet we run into limits, which emerge above all from the closets of our experience: Without common experience we cannot translate. Shades of color cannot be communicated to a blind person, nor the experience of the sea to the tropical forest dweller. Each word exists in and refers to a certain network of correspondences. The cohesion of the network cannot be captured fully by words from a different network. Nevertheless, we must penetrate the other networks, to understand and describe them with the connections of our own network. Similarly, another language with its connotations is not fully amenable to being expressed in our own, for we never carry over the whole world view, which gives the images their meaning. Marie von Ebner-Eschenbach even believes that...the spirit of a language manifests itself most clearly in its untranslatable words.

This is not the end of the question. For what happens to law, which lives in and through a language, when it is translated?[2] Inasmuch as the structure and significance of the language shape thought, the language determines the construction and content of law. Legal sentences hence change their content if they are delivered in another language, in another network of connotations and thereby in another "form of life" (Wittgenstein), in another "field of force" (Quine). The farther languages and the underlying life experience diverge from each other, the greater the alteration can be. ......

Prejudice

The difficulty consists in that we perceive the foreign order through the "eyeglasses" of our world experience, our language, our linguistic understandings: We hearken to a foreign conch, and take our own pulse beat to be the roar of the world sea. But what are the contents of foreign symbols? Methods of interpretation, tried and true in our language, may lead us into error in other languages and other symbolic systems.

It becomes especially dangerous if we become familiar with the external symbols. Do they stand for the same content? How do they relate to each other? How is the surrounding area of silence? Is the symbol intended as concrete or abstract; does it represent a fact or an idea? Is it supposed to simulate a regulation (for example, a "western" standard—as to some extent in China and Japan?); is it supposed to operate only rhetorically?

The danger of misunderstanding is great in comparative law, as here too we naturally are fixated on words; hence, we begin with texts as sources. Comparative law in the European style is from its

---

2. The original German plays on the German word for "translate" ("*übersetzen*"), which is composed of the German words for "set over," by introducing a hyphen into the normally unhyphenated word: *i.e., "über-setzt."*

cultural markings actually "language-conditional," "language-trusting" — as we have seen. But how reliable is that with respect to other cultures? We may miss the mark of a foreign system if we look to legal words or legal texts. Language may count as less "systematizing" abroad; its relation to reality may be different. How can we determine its position?

Warning

We may not in any case expect in another culture the specific "language-trust" of our own culture. Consequently, a "language-trusting" comparative law runs into limitations, particularly when it encounters a "language-mistrustful" culture. (Who still trusts words in the States of the Eastern bloc?) In addition, a foreign language may render with precision or more likely "create atmosphere;" it also can be less exact:

> The Chinese language clearly is not intended for the recording of concepts, for the analysis of thoughts, for the representation of precepts. It is, rather, totally cut out for the communication of intuitive views, for the suggestion of a certain mode of behavior, for persuasion and conversion.

We need to know the entire code of the relevant culture in order to understand its "language transmission." Applicable to comparative law in any case is: "It is impossible for me to value the word so highly." (Goethe, *Faust I*).

Even with respect to the value of our point of departure, "language," and "text," we thus need to be careful, indeed *very* careful.

As we have seen, rules of conduct generally are only in part made known through language; what is most important often remains "between the lines," "between one word and another." The silent space between words is of different breadth in different cultures. Words "swim" on an "ocean" of silence; they relate to a common, silent background. When we read texts in foreign languages, frequently we do not take into account this different manner of silence; instead, we project our own "silence" into the text, thus bringing it into a different meaning network. For this reason, the reading of a foreign legal text often yields an incorrect image; misunderstanding is programmed.

In order to avoid this, we must recognize the text's surroundings. Yet we cannot observe the surroundings mentally, for every system reacts to observation, and observes itself. As in the natural sciences, social reality differs according to whether we observe it or not:

"What happens depends on how we observe the observed, or at least from the fact that we observe."

The "poverty of a system" lies for example almost never in the used and manifest books for internal use; only rarely do we read something through to the way it is accomplished in practice. We thus always remain in danger of taking incorrectly the represented for life, and dead law for living law.

Autonomy of Language

Also important for comparison is how independent language is. Does it have intrinsic value (*Rechtstaat*) or is it merely a tool in the hands of the powerful? In our country, in principle, language is advanced by the state: Society gives names ("man gave names to all cattle, and to the birds of the heavens...," (Genesis 2.20) *(vox populi, vox dei)*, the state does not rule over ideas (cf. Art. 5, GG): "*Caesar non supra grammaticos!*" The courtier Marcellus is reputed to have answered Emperor Tiberius (42 B.C.–37 A.D.): "Civil rights you can give to people, Emperor, but not words." That actually is not undisputed (cf., for example, "Language regulations" in dictatorships or the manipulation of language in the socialist commando economy ["*Kommandowirtschaft*"] , but, rather, a matter of fundamental European agreement.

In China, it is otherwise: the first emperor of a Chinese centralized state, Quin Shihuang (3rd century B.C.), erected a monument with the following inscription: "He regulates all things, he considers all deeds. He gave to all things the right names."

He who possesses political power decides what *is* true; he can and may regulate language; he is unconstrained by words, laws and rights. He who can name things rules them. Erwin Wickert reports as follows:

> The Chancellor Cha Gao, who wanted to usurp the throne, made a test of strength. He presented a deer to the emperor, and said that he was giving him this horse as a gift. The emperor laughed: 'I think you misspoke, Mr. Chancellor? That is no horse, but a deer!' But when he turned to the officials and courtiers, in order that they support him, his laughter died. They had serious expressions, and pondered intensely. Some were of the opinion that the animal indeed appeared in certain respects, and depending on the perspective from which one viewed it, not totally unlike a horse. Some could not make up their minds. Yet oth-

ers unhesitatingly saw in the deer nothing other than a deer, and said so frankly. The Chancellor had them punished.

That was the end of the second emperor. He no longer was able to name things. He possessed no power over them. Power had passed to the Chancellor, who forced the emperor to take poison, and thus ended the dynasty.

Reality Reference

Above all, we do not know *how* a foreign language invokes reality: "Every word is a word of oath. Whichever spirit does the summoning — such a one appears."

Each culture summons something else, and it echoes back differently.

Even with identical texts of law in the same language, outcomes can diverge. The partially differing interpretations of the *Code civil* in France and Belgium is a classic example; the application of the civil law in the Federal Republic of Germany and the former DDR is a sad example. From the similitude of the statutory law flows no similarity of the life of the law.

Equality

To give order to connections and to render them comprehensible also is *the* scholarly duty of comparative law. To systematize signifies for us "to recognize what is equal." The "equality of the application of law" thus means for us the "soul of justice" (*equal justice under the law*) [original in English]. Yet once again we encounter the barrier of language; for language brings certain parts into prominence and thereby achieves "equality." It conveys to us the meaning of what is salutary and just: "Language serves to communicate the useful and the harmful and thus also what is just and unjust." (Aristotle, *Politics*).

We use the word "*Spannung*" ("tension/excitement") for the mental domain ("I await with excitement" [*"Spannung"* in German], as well as for the electrical current ("high voltage") [*"Hochspannung"* in German], and thus fabricate a relation of equality of dubious reality. A similar result obtains if we equate man and property through the concepts "natural person" and "legal person" — although one is visible while the other is invisible.

Language thus conveys equality; in it the equally designated appear as analogous: "The equality of the moment captured in the word allows all otherwise heterogeneity of the intuitive content to retreat more and more, and finally causes it to disappear altogether.

Here too a part thereby takes the position of the whole, even becomes and is the whole."

That is the *"pars pro toto"* as the fundamental principle of linguistic metaphor and a medium for conveying equality. Examples thereof are to fly = birds; Russia = (formerly) USSR; Holland = the Netherlands; England = the United Kingdom. Through the highlighting of parts, language conveys a commonality between "different" matters ("principle of equivalence"); individual parts tie together other totalities as "equal": Highly different contents can "be handled equally in language, such that every assertion, which derives meaning from one, extends to another and is transferred."

Conversely, language hinders equality relations [:]....the term "embryo" instead of "unborn child" "facilitates" abortion ("infanticide" does not fit). Language thus determines equality or inequality, life and death.

Languages function differently in this regard, each creating different equalities. A few cultures, for example, count butterflies as birds, because they fly....We must track down these different "equivalences" if we wish to understand foreign values.

Along with this, cultures value equal treatment differently as a claim to justice. Languages can emphasize equality ("you" [*i.e.,* the fact that English does not distinguish between the familiar and polite by having different forms of the pronoun in the second person], but also distance ("Du," "Sie" [in German, the former signaling familiarity and intimacy; the latter, politeness and distance] or inequality ("he"). By these means, they create an image of that which is "natural." In addition, the equality construction—especially as "chance equality"—collides with family thinking and group thinking. Families and groups are just as "natural," just as "just" and just as determinative of structure: it is then an ethical mission, not corruption, to privilege family members.

Abstract / Concrete

We also must separate languages that privilege the abstract expression from those that emphasize the concrete. For example, Chinese has no word for "old man," yet has many expressions for aspects of old age; similarly, in Japanese, the general concepts of "beauty' and "justice" seem to be nonexistent. Abstraction produces the equality fusion; equality exists only in the abstract: the more abstract, the more "equal"!

Language-supported differences can achieve a remoteness in our law that we can reduce only with patience, but can not eliminate.

Thus we find ourselves once again before the question of if and how the language of law captures reality: "If, for example, the same ideas and words are found in two different systems, and are defined differently in relation to their mutual connections, in what sense can one still say that these ideas represent reality?"

(b) *Questions*

1. What makes some words untranslatable? Are those attributes constants for all words, perhaps at differing levels of intensity?

2. What does Professor Großfeld signal as being the danger of symbols?

3. In which ways can symbols be separated from the symbolized? In which ways can they not be?

4. What is the importance of silence in language, or, as Professor Großfeld puts it, of "the silent space between words"? How is this relevant to law?

3. *Translation's Alchemy*[3]

(a) Vivian Grosswald Curran, *Cultural Immersion*
46 American Journal of Comparative Law pp. 54–59

III. Comparative Law as a Phenomenon of Translation

Comparative law in the United States is taught in English, with translations of foreign-language legal texts. n32 Translation illustrates the inseparability of law and language, and the field of translation is an extraordinarily rich source for insights into the process of comparison. The comparative act inevitably is a form of translation, illustrative of both the potentials for communicating the new and the pitfalls for betraying or losing the original in a process of transmutation. n33 Translation also operates within languages, among the plurality of discourses embedded in what passes for one language, and is merely more apparent in the international arena where the distinctions among the discourses called languages are official.

---

3. See Hoffman, infra note 39.

n34 The multitude of discourses that actually coexist within a given official legal culture illustrates that many cultures can be said to exist within the boundaries of a given legal system, a condition implicitly recognized in the comparatist joke that the United States and England are two countries separated by a common law and a common language. n35

The untranslatable, in the largest sense of the word, remains the biggest challenge for the legal comparatist. It is the challenge of immersing oneself with sufficient depth into a foreign legal culture so as to assess it from within.n36 Fluency in the target culture's language is one aspect of immersion. n37 The degree of comparatists' intimacy with the target culture's language is one measure of the degree of their cultural immersion. In his 1995 inaugural address at Oxford, the comparatist and philosopher of language, George Steiner, urging the need for comparatists to know many foreign languages, discussed how complicated even the concept of translation is. He told the story of Roman Jakobson, the great Russian-born structural linguist, who was reputed to have known seventeen languages, "but," according to Steiner, "all in Russian!" n38 .

In structuralist parlance, the problem of translation is that it is ill-suited to finding sign equivalents that include both the signifier and the signified. As Eva Hoffman, the author of a book about the connections between language and world view, puts it,

> the problem [with a foreign word translation] is that the signifier is severed from the signified. The words I learn now don't stand for things in the same unquestioned way they did in my native tongue. "River" in Polish was a vital sound, energized with the essence of riverhood, of my rivers, of my being immersed in rivers. "Rivers" in English is cold—a word without an aura. It has no accumulated associations for me...It does not evoke....I try laboriously to translate not from English to Polish but from the word back to its source, to the feeling from which it springs....This radical disjoining between word and thing is a dessicating alchemy, draining the world not only of significance but of its colors, striations, nuances—its very existence. It is the loss of a living connection. n39

There is a French adage according to which all translation is betrayal. The adage is itself untranslatable because its effect in French comes in part from the similarity in sound between the French words for "translate" and "betray" which the adage unites on both a semantic and a phonic level: *traduire c'est trahir*. But we should remember that the word "betrayal" has two meanings, one connoting treachery, but the other connoting revelation, or the seeping through of some thing which cannot be disguised. Each language renders a whole world view, and translation means uniting two different world views. The target language may betray the original by failing to offer its connotative attributes, the multiplicity of signifieds that underlie each signifier, but it is also the first step in betraying at least something of the novelty of the original text, and thereby extending the arena of communication and the possibilities for understanding. n40

Translations from formal language to formal language, from discourse to discourse, and from connotation or referential sources of concepts from one legal culture to another, all involve categorization. When translating, one discovers that one transmits only a portion of the original. n41 Generally one selects among various possible subsets of the original, making value judgments as to which aspects of the original sign should be preserved through triage. The text in translation will trigger associations based on those selections, but they will be associations often not present in the original text, triggered by the signifiers used in the translation, such that a transmutation occurs from the original, making the translation a new and distinct product.

Perception is dependent on the prism through which the observer observes, such that the outsiders-translators' access to the original will be compromised by their not being of the culture which produced the original text. n42 While the prisms that are our *biological-cum-*cultural baggage clearly limit our perception, they are, how ever, also the very mechanisms which enable us to see. The absence of prisms would not be unfettered vision, but void. Bio-cultural particularities thus both restrict our experiential and learning capacity in a channeling or filtering process, and, on the other hand, are the very means by which we can learn at all. n43

The immersion approach in comparative legal analysis suggests the importance of trying to understand foreign legal cultures in an untranslated form; *i.e.,* through the prisms that shape perceptions in the target legal culture. This implies both an expansion and alteration of the comparatist's prisms. The immersion approach ideally involves an expansion of perceptual prisms rather than an exchange. In other words, the original legal culture should be viewed in untranslated form, but comparatists need to retain their stance as outsiders even as they acquire insight into the insiders' view. Otherwise, they will fail to perceive with sufficient acuity those fundamental, powerful aspects of target legal cultures which are so entrenched as to be unarticulated and even unconscious. As Steiner writes, "learning [is] the suspension of reflex." n44

Comparatists cannot hope to perceive beyond the limits of their perceptions, nor to divest themselves entirely of the substructural categorizations of their own cultures of origin. The questions comparatists ask will reflect their own perceptual prisms and affect their receptivity to data from observed legal cultures: "Subjects or fields of study are determined by the kinds of questions to which they have been invented to provide the answers." n45 This means that the comparatist will fail to grasp a foreign legal culture completely from within, like Edward Saïd's exiles who are "migrants and perhaps hybrids in, but not of, any situation in which [they] find themselves." n46 The benefits lie in illuminating the observed legal culture in ways that are new for those within it, and in providing valuable insights for the comparatist as well, both about the target legal culture and the culture of origin. n47 In *Law's Empire*, Ronald Dworkin makes the point that interpretation in fields such as law inevitably is concerned with purpose, and that the purposes are those of the interpreter. He writes that "constructive interpretation is a matter of imposing pur pose on an object or practice," and defines creative interpretation as a "matter of interaction between purpose and subject." n48 This definition illustrates the dynamic nature of the comparative act, through which both interpreter and interpreted can learn, and whose product leaves neither unchanged.

Law itself is one of many categorizations subject to challenge, inasmuch as it suggests a severance from other fields, such as politics, history, economics, anthropology and language, that nevertheless are inextricably connected to the law in mutually defining relationships.n49 The immersion approach signifies the need to cross traditional disciplinary lines, and to challenge the integrity of the traditional definition of law. In other words, it suggests that law does not have a life of its own.

NOTES

n32. European law schools have started to offer substantive law courses on foreign legal systems taught in the target countries' languages, and at least one French law school, Cergy-Pontoise, offers an entire law school curriculum in English and German. In the United States, I am aware of only the following substantive law courses in foreign languages: courses in Latin American law taught in Spanish at Columbia University, St. Mary's and the University of Florida; and a Japanese research course taught in Japanese at N.Y.U. Law School. I have started a "Foreign Languages for Lawyers" program at the University of Pittsburgh, where I developed a curriculum of French taught in a legal context. We now also offer German, Spanish and Chinese for Lawyers, modeled on the French course, and this year for the first time are opening the classes to practicing lawyers. My hope is that these courses eventually will be a first step to teaching substantive law courses on the target countries' legal systems in the target languages, with the use of bilingual materials both to continue the language-acquisition benefits of the beginning courses, and to facilitate reading for students. See Curran, "Developing and Teaching a Foreign-Language Course for Law Students," 43 J. Legal Educ. 598 (1993); and Vivian Grosswald Curran, Learning French Through the Law: A Comparative French/English Treatment of Terms in a Legal Context (1996). We have to date not been able to progress beyond the initial languages-for-lawyers courses.

n33. Significantly, the classical Latin term for metaphor was *translatio*, which the Roman rhetorician Quintilian described as "shining forth with a light that is all its own." Marius Fabius Quintilianus, Institutio Oratoria 303 (H.E. Butler, trans. 1954).

n34. See Steiner, supra n. 10, at 151 (emphasis added) ("this... process... becomes fully visible...across language barriers.").

n35. See Balkin, supra n. 9, at 1229 ("Language is perhaps the most prominent form of collective cultural software.")

n36. See Claude Levi-Strauss, Structural Anthropology (Claire Jacobson & Brooke Grundfest Schoepf trans. 1963). See also von Humboldt, "Über die Verschiedenheit des menschlichen Sprachbanes," quoted in Pierre Petitgirard, Du Langage 159 (1976) (*"chaque langage offre une vision du monde particulière"*).

n37. My argument here dovetails, but is distinct from, the deconstructionist view that language is the cause of the alteration between world and expression (between referent and sign), and that language use is an interpretive act, rather than an act that reflects or mirrors. Deconstruction's insights into the inadequacies of language implicate comparative law and, more generally, law and legal analysis inasmuch as communication and analysis are fundamentallytranslation. See id., quoting Emile Benveniste (*"Nous pensons un univers que notre langue a d'abord modelé."*)

n38. Steiner, supra n. 10, at 153.

n39. Eva Hoffman, Lost in Translation: A Life in a New Language 106–07 (1989). See also The Silence of Polyglots in Kristeva, supra n. 13, at 13, on what it means to be bereft of one's mother-tongue through exile. Cf. Jacques Derrida, Marges de la Philosophie 1 (1972): "*Penser son autre: cela revient-il seulement à relever (aufheben) ce dont elle relève...?*"; and Layoun, "Cultural Transgression and Tribute," in Between Languages and Cultures: Translation and Cross-Cultural Texts 267, 268 (Anuradha Dingwaney, et al. eds., 1995) ("Translation [is] a multivalent configuration of the attempt to make familiar ... the strange and silent,...the inapprehensible, and...the drawn-near"; and Noam Chomsky, Syntactic Structures (1957) on similar paradigms within a language, rather than across languages, and for the idea that language has limits because it has structure. See also Ryan, "The Convention on Contracts for the International Sale of Goods: Divergent Interpretations," 4 Tul. J. Int'l. & Comp. L. 99, 116 (1995) (Discussion of problems arising from six official language-versions of an international convention.)

n40. James Boyd White captures the duality of translation when he defines translation as failure, but as "failure of a most instructive kind." James Boyd White, Justice as Translation 255 (1990) (emphasis added). Alan Watson's analysis of legal borrowings or "transplants" illustrates the element of creation embedded in the trans lation process. See Watson, "Aspects of Reception of Law," 44 Am. J. Comp. L. 335, 345–46 (1996); and George Steiner, After Babel: Aspects of Language and Translation (2d ed. 1992).

n41. See Eike von Savigny, The Social Foundations of Meaning 78 (1988). See also Steiner, supra n. 9, at 326 ("[A] language act is inexhaustible to interpretation precisely because its context is the world.")

n42. Here I use "text" in the broadest possible sense. Cf. Jacques Derrida, Of Grammatology 163 (Gayadri Chakravorky Spivak trans. 1976) ("*il n'y a pas de hors-texte.*") See also George P. Fletcher, Basic Concepts of Legal Thought (1966) for penetrating insights into the challenges of translating basic legal concepts from one language to another; Nadelmann & von Mehren, supra n. 12; Favoreu, "American and European Models of Justice," in Comparative and Private International Law, supra n. 5, at 105; Reimann, "German Legal Science," 31 B.C. L. Rev. 837, 895, on "shared... terminology but not...meaning"; and Quine, supra n. 14, at ix ("Studies of the semantics of reference consequently turn out to make sense only when directed upon substantially our language, from within.") For an excellent analysis of both the similarities and the distinctions between translations and interpretations, see White, supra n. 40, at 236–46.

n43. See Hans-Georg Gadamer, Truth and Method 245 (Joel Weinsheimer et al., trans., 1995) (1975) for the crucial role of linguistic and historical situatedness in opening new dimensions and horizons, as well as for the positive value of prejudice. Thus, the comparatist's enterprise is not merely to unearth and dismantle unwarranted prejudices in target legal cultures, but to appreciate that 'what appears to be a limiting prejudice from the viewpoint of... reason in fact belongs to historical reality itself." Id. at 277. See also Balkin, supra n. 9, at 1232; and Norman N. Holland, The Critical I, 41–53 (1992) ("I use codes.... I cannot speak without them. I cannot speak except in their language. In that sense, they 'speak through' me. Yet in no sense need one assume that they make the I disappear. Just the opposite. The codes demand an I to run them.")

n44. Steiner, supra n. 9, at 26. Alan Watson states the converse with equal succinctness: "We are blinkered by what we know." Watson, supra n. 31, at 444.

n45. Isaiah Berlin, Concepts and Categories: Philosophical Essays 1 (1978). See also Hyland, "Comparative Law," in A Companion to the Philosophy of Law and Legal Theory 184 (Dennis Patterson, ed. 1996); Gadamer, supra n. 43, at 374 ("The close relation between questioning and understanding is what gives the hermeneutic experience its true dimension"); and Connes, supra n. 12, at 51 ("We can... ask to what extent physical truth depends on which question we put to nature, that is, which experiments we choose to carry out.") This is also true of analysis within a given culture. See Balkin, "A Night in the Topics: The Reason of Legal Rhetoric and the Rhetoric of Legal Reason," in Law Stories: Narrative and Rhetoric in the Law 215 (Peter Brooks & Paul Gewirtz, eds. 1996) ("topics undergird invention and discovery"); and Felix Cohen, The Legal Conscience 466–71 (the importance of Plato, Hegel, and Marx lies in the questions they formulated).

n46. Edward Saïd, After the Last Sky: Palestinian Lives 164 (1985) (emphasis added).

n47. For an illustration of a "translation" within a given culture, see George Lakoff, Moral Politics: What Conservatives Know that Liberals Don't (1996) (Presenting the thesis that conservative and liberal political positions in the United States have a metaphoric derivation based on two different, opposing views of the family. Lakoff posits that Americans unconsciously understand nationhood in terms of a metaphor that conflates the concept of nation with that of family, yielding conservatives who embrace a strict father model, while liberals embrace a nurturing parent model.) Cf. Clifford Geertz, Local Knowledge 84 (1983) ("Common sense is not what the mind cleared of cant spontaneously apprehends; it is what the mind filled with presuppositions... concludes.")

n48. Ronald Dworkin, Law's Empire 52 (1986). Accord, Jerome Hall, Comparative Law and Social Theory 82 (1963). Cf. Rodolfo Sacco in Pierre Legrand, "Questions à Rodolfo Sacco," 4 R.I.D.C. 943, 949 (1995) ("The comparatist's teaching necessarily favors some values over others. But only the comparatist who cheats establishes in advance the values to be favored.")

n49. Significantly, "law" is a term not easily amenable to translation from English, the language of common law legal culture, to the languages of the civil law legal cultures. See Fletcher, supra n. 42, at 28–40 (analyzing different substantive meanings of the term "law" in different legal systems, and in particular contrasting the unitary use of the term "law" in the common law systems, with the use of two terms in civil law systems). See also Legrand, supra n. 18, at 52, 58 ("It has to be understood that the 'legal' cannot be analytically separated from the 'non-legal' of society...").

(b) *Questions*

1. What processes of translation also are involved in comparative law?

2. How does comparative legal analysis mirror legal analysis generally?

3. What is the relevance to comparative law of George Steiner's statement that "learning [is] the suspension of reflex?"

IV. Comparison by Cultural Immersion

1. *Introduction*

The authors of the following excerpts believe that comparing is essential to understanding. They also believe that understanding a legal phenomenon requires deep penetration into the world that produced the phenomenon, a process described as "cultural immersion."

The first essay presents a theoretical view of the meaning and role of comparative analysis, while the second and third provide concrete instantiations of comparative analysis through cultural immersion.

2. *The Nature and Necessity of Comparison*

(a) Vivian Grosswald Curran, *Cultural Immersion*
46 American Journal of Comparative Law 43, 46–54 1998)

The goals and purposes of comparative legal studies have been various. They have included the functional ascertainment of practical solutions to legal problems in one or more legal systems, an understanding of foreign legal systems, and a deeper understanding of one's own legal system. To this list should be added, I suggest, the enrichment of our understanding of the process of legal analysis, for comparative law highlights an analytical process present in all legal analysis. It is merely more visible in the area of comparative law, where national borders and languages underscore the presence of a comparative paradigm that otherwise would not be apparent.

The point that comparative analysis is integral to all legal analysis is often unrecognized for two reasons. First, the traditional Western view treats identity as a foundational concept, and difference as a derivative concept, such that one can say that two things are different only if one can say that they are not the same. n3 Difference, however, is equally as foundational a concept as identity, because it is only by illustrating difference that identity is possible, and neither has meaning outside of a comparative paradigm. Any definition, explanation, or constitutive description depends on the existence of an *other*, such that the concept of any *a* is meaningless without the concept of a *non-a*. It is, therefore, not just legal comparatists, whose occupation with the different, the *other*, is manifest, who must engage in comparison, but also all legal scholars seeking to analyze and identify attributes of their own legal systems. n4

Secondly, the difficulty of perceiving the ubiquity of the comparative act is due to the fact that traditional categories of legal analysis obfuscate differences within those categories. Distinct legal discourses within legal systems, like those of the young and the old, men and women, the uneducated and the educated, the poor and the wealthy, have tended to be undifferentiated under traditional categorizations, such as the United States' legal system, the French legal system, common law, civil law, and so on. n5 Distinct discourses even exist between any two individuals attempting to communicate with each other, such that the communicator formulates a communication that the addressee transforms, however subtly, in a process that passes for understanding. n6 The cognitive sciences suggest that each individual's cognition depends on comparison, because human under standing is a function of relating one entity or domain to another. n7 Thus, within each official legal system, and between any two interlocutors, a comparative process is needed to render one person's or group's discourse intelligible to another person or group.

The following three concepts and their corollaries are central to my thesis: (1) Categorization is crucial to our perceptions and understanding of data, and the categories we erect result from our experience and in turn affect our perceptions and, therefore, our experiences. Categories vary from culture to culture. n8 Experience in turn is a combination of our cultural contexts and our physical makeup. n9 (2) The comparative act is part and parcel of understanding and reasoning, of the very process of cognition, such that, being automatic, it often goes unnoticed. n10 (3) One of the consequences of cognition's dependence on comparison is an inevitable and endless paradigm of transmutation, of a concept's alteration through the comparative process.

Corollaries of element (3) are (a) the primacy and persistence of difference; and (b) the inevitability of distortion in the comparative act. Difference persists and characterizes the comparative act inasmuch as, by definition, comparison involves at least two distinct entities or domains. In other words, comparison fails to establish exact equivalences or identities. n11

Distortion prevails in the impossibility of completely understanding one domain in terms of another. By virtue of being "other," the second will have only certain properties in common with the first, such that focusing on the second domain as a way of conceptualizing the first will result in suppressing certain properties of the first, as it will mean highlighting others. Distortion also prevails at a more fundamental level. Each person's cultural context is unique to some extent, such that no two people's understanding of a concept will be identical in any discourse outside of purely symbolic ones, such as that of mathematics. It has also been proposed that a word never has the same meaning twice, neither when used more than once by the same person, nor when used by different people. n12

This does not mean that communication is impossible. It means, rather, that communication is doomed to imperfection. Perfect communication by means of human language would require that all interlocutors have identical cultural backgrounds and physical makeups. n13 Difficulties in transmitting concepts across cultural-linguistic differences are related to the level of abstraction connoted by the words in question. Divergences of meaning lessen to the extent that language corresponds to what Quine calls "nonverbal stimulation": objects amenable to visible or tactile perception. n14 Thus, while two people from different legal cultures may diverge little in their understandings of the words "the ocean liner Queen Elizabeth II," they will diverge far more in their understandings of such terms as "contract," "judicial opinion," or "liability." n15 The possibilities for effective communication increase the more interlocutors share in terms of their cultural contexts. n16 Thus, a valid examination of another legal culture requires immersion into the political, historical, economic and linguistic contexts that molded the legal system, and in which the legal system operates. n17 It requires an explanation of various cultural mentalities, to adapt a term from the French concept of an *histoire des mentalités*. n18 I advocate this approach, which I will call the cultural immersion approach, as a prerequisite for effective comparative legal analysis.

The cultural immersion approach is similar to what other scholars have started to advocate in a variety of forms. Robert Cover refers to a "narrative nomos"; n19 Hans-Georg Gadamer to "pre-understanding"; n20 Günter Frankenberg to "the unconscious spell that holds us to see others by the measure of ourselves"; n21 Bernhard Großfeld to "joint experience"; n22 Jürgen Habermas to "an intersubjectively shared context of possible understanding"; n23 Pierre Legrand to a "socio-cognitive context"; n24 Willard Quine to "intersubjectively available cues"; n25 and Janet Ainsworth to "culturally contingent normative baggage." n26 Similarly, William Ewald's reference to "comparative jurisprudence" evokes an immersion process to discover, from within, the thoughts of others in other places and times. n27 In the contemporary generation, postmodernist theory has inspired ideas such as immersion, and has begun to influence scholarship in areas of legal study such as feminist jurisprudence, critical race theory and constitutional law. Postmodernist theories have influenced legal theory in recent years by, among others, suggesting the relevance to law of other fields, such as anthropology, psychology, linguistics, philosophy and sociology, and have promoted new perceptions of and challenges to the fundamental traditional categories in law.

The immersion approach is, however, by no means original to this generation of legal comparatists. The generation of comparatists who led comparative legal studies in American law schools for the last half century also practiced the immersion approach, but *sub silentio*, without fanfare, and as the most intuitively obvious of methodological necessities. They were to a large extent a generation of émigrés from Hitler's Europe, and were uniquely well situated to engage in cultural immersion because they were, to varying degrees, of at least two legal cultures; because they knew foreign languages, often numerous languages including Latin and Greek; and because the breadth of their historico-cultural knowledge spanned many fields, making them interdisciplinarians *avant la lettre*, n28 like the *bourgeois gentilhomme* of Molière who was told by his fancy tutor that he spoke in prose when he thought he was merely speaking in French. n29 Thus, the émigré generation had no need to construct a formal methodological theory of immersion, let alone to arrive at one based on postmodernist or other philosophy. Being of two countries, and sometimes more, the comparatist scholars of the last generation understood that translating from one legal discourse to another requires an understanding of the respective legal cultures.

If the current generation has begun to feel obliged to articulate the necessity of a contextual or cultural immersion approach to comparative legal analysis, it is not because such a methodology would be an innovation. On the contrary, it is because the generation of émigré comparatists is retiring and dying, leaving comparative law in the United States to be taught by stop-gap, short-term visiting professors from abroad or by native-born American professors generally bereft of effective foreign-language skills. n30 The scope of native-born American comparatists' cultural, literary, historical, social and political knowledge of civil-law systems generally pales in comparison with the vast background of the classically educated European émigrés who, to borrow a phrase George Steiner once used in tribute to Robert Musil, so often seemed to carry all of Western civilization in their minds.

In my view, the émigré generation excelled at subtlety of feeling for the nuances of the civil and common law systems, but, as will be more fully discussed below, purposely privileged findings of sameness and underestimated the significance of differences. The risks of erroneous conclusions will only increase if contemporary comparatists continue this approach, but with less of an intuitive understanding than their predecessors possessed of the workings and shades of meaning of the relevant cultures. The challenge we face today is to (1) salvage comparative law in the United States for the future by identifying and fostering the crucial attributes needed for engaging in it effectively; and (2) to demarginalize it within legal academic curricula so as to offer our students a clearer view of the depths of under lying differences and similarities among legal cultures, the contingent nature of their own legal culture, and the analysis they should be conducting in all subjects of their legal studies in translating the foreign into the familiar. n31

NOTES

n3. See Jacques Derrida, Writing and Difference 278–79 (1978); Jacques Derrida, Margins of Philosophy 3–27 (trans. Alan Bass, 1982).; Balkin, "Deconstructive Practice and Legal Theory," 96 Yale L.J. 743, 748–49 (1987); Minow, "In Context," 63 S. Cal. L. Rev. 1597, 1600 (1990) (defining all contexts as "patterns of difference"); Mi now, supra n. 1; Balkin, "The Hohfeldian Approach to Law and Semiotics," 44 U. of Miami L. Rev. 1119 (1990); and Maurice Merleau-Ponty, Signs 39 (Richard C. Mc Cleary, trans., 1964) ("Taken singly, signs do not specify anything, and...each one of them does not so much express a meaning as mark a divergence of meaning between itself and other signs. Since the same can be said for all other signs, we may conclude that language is made up of differences without terms; or more exactly, that the terms of language are engendered only by the differences which appear among them.") Cf., Legrand, "The Impossibility of Legal Transplants," 4 Maastricht J. Eur. & Comp. L. 123 (1997) ("comparison must involve 'the primary and fundamental investigation of difference'").

n4. Cf. Balkin & Levinson, "Constitutional Grammar," 72 Tex. L. Rev. 1771, 1779 (1994) ("To justify an existing practice, or to argue about how the practice could be better carried out, one must turn to a different practice and the arguments of justification available within it."); and Paul Ricœur, Le Conflit des interprétations 20 (1969) (Defining hermeneutics as "an understanding of oneself by the circuity of understanding the other"); and Goodrich, "Poor Illiterate Reason: History, Nationalism and Common Law," 1 Social & Legal Studies 7, 10 (1992) ("the identity of a nation, and so of a constitution and law, is a negative product. It is a cultural artifact built against, and distinctive by nature of its opposition to, other national traditions and other laws.") Gödel's theorem states a similar principle, applicable to the natural sciences: namely, that "the consistency of a logical system cannot be proven within the system." Jean-Pierre Changeux & Alain Connes, Conversations on Mind, Matter and Mathematics 241 (M.B. Debevoise, ed. & trans., 1995).

n5. I refer here to the plurality of unofficial legal discourses. On the existence of a "stubborn and persistent formal pluralism" of legal discourses, see Lawrence M. Friedman, Some Thoughts on Comparative Legal Culture in Comparative and Private International Law: Essays in Honor of John Henry Merriman, 49, 52 (David S. Clark ed., 1990). See also Fuller, "Positivism and Fidelity to Law: A Reply to Professor Hart," 71 Harv. L. Rev. 630, 668, n.40 (1958) (there are "countless informal and over lapping systems that run through language as a whole.")

n6. See George Steiner, After Babel (2d ed. 1992); George Lakoff, Women, Fire and Dangerous Things: What Categories Reveal About the Mind (1987); and Curran, "Metaphor Is the Mother of All Law," in Law and The Conflict of Ideologies (Roberta Kevelson ed., 1995).

n7. See Lakoff, supra n. 6; George Lakoff & Mark Johnson, Metaphors We Live By (1980). For a report on contemporary research into category-based cognition, see George Johnson, "What Happens When the Brain Can't Remember," New York Times, Sunday, July 7, 1996, at 10.

n8. A related question which I do not discuss in this article is how categories evolve and change within a legal culture. For an illustration of this process in the evolution of legal theory from naturalism to positivism to modernism, see Alcantara, "Ideology, Historiography and International Legal Theory," 9 Int. J. For the Semiotics of Law 39–79 (1996). For an analysis of "systematic evolution [in the European Union as] self-referential and resulting from the internal dynamics of the system itself..." see Weiler, "The Transformation of Europe," 100 Yale L.J. 2403, 2410 (1991).

n9. Another way to put this is to say that experience is "embodied". See Lakoff, supra n. 6. A generation before Lakoff coined the term "embodied experience," George Steiner was referring to a similar concept as an "intricate congruence of innate and environmental options." George Steiner, On Difficulty and Other Essays 2 (1978) (1972). Accord, Balkin, "Ideology as Cultural Software," 16 Cardozo L. Rev. 1221, 1228 (1995). ("To exist as a person is to exist as a person who is part biological hard ware and part cultural software. The two together constitute the person....")

n10. Lakoff discusses metaphor as being intrinsic to human cognitive processes, rather than simile, the rhetorical technique traditionally associated with comparison. His use of the term metaphor, however, includes comparison in the sense that I use it; i.e., the inevitability of understanding one phenomenon in terms of another, and the failure to establish complete identity between any two domains. I do not use the term comparison in order to contrast it with conflation, the process traditionally associated with metaphor. Despite the traditional view of metaphor as establishing equivalence, it does not establish complete identity. Its power lies, rather, in the comparative act by which one domain is illuminated through another, a process that involves selecting attributes common to both and, therefore, suppressing others. See Lakoff, supra n. 6; Lakoff & Johnson, supra n. 7; Steiner, "What is Comparative Literature?," in No Passion Spent, Essays: 1978–1995, 143 (1996) ("It may well be that the reflexes that put in play similarity and dissimilarity, analogy and contrast are fundamental to the human psyche and to the possibility of the intelligible. French makes this audible: in 'reason,' raison, 'comparison,' comparaison, is instrumental."); and Curran, supra n. 6. Aristotle categorized metaphor as a variant of comparison: "The simile...is a metaphor, differing from it only in that the simile adds the phrase of comparison...and...the hearer does not have to seek the resemblance." Aristotle, The Rhetoric of Aristotle 207 (Lane Cooper, trans. 1932).

n11. I use identities here to mean both that which is identical and that which is definitional, or identity-giving.

n12. See Van Den Bergh, "Jacob Israel De Haan's Legal Significs," 9 Int.J. for the Semiotics of Law 81, 86 (1996). For centuries, however, it was thought that a perfect, essentialist language was achievable, a language whose words would name objects in the world without room for ambiguity, like the language that the Bible says God gave Adam before the confusion at Babel. Esperanto represents a modern attempt to devise a perfect language. For a thorough and fascinating history of this centuries-old search that reveals much about changing human conceptions of life, see Umberto Eco, The Search for the Perfect Language (1995), ("The history of the reasons why Europe thought that it needed a perfect language can...tell us a good deal about the cultural history of that continent." Id. at 19.) A contemporary disbeliever in the possibility of a universal language is the philosopher Aviezer Ravitzky ("While I believe the human spirit is universal, I don't believe it can be expressed in a universal language. If we don't have roots, then we will never have flowers." Quoted in Emily Hauser, "Out of Eden," Inside 19 (1995). See also Nadelmann & von Mehren, "Equivalences in Treaties in the Conflicts Field," 15 Am. J. Comp. L. 195, 195 (1967) (The same terms can have different meanings within one language in different legal systems.)

The possibility of a language capable of perfectly representing the world was rejected implicitly by J. L. Austin, as it was by Wittgenstein. For the argument against a perfect legal language, see also Lionel Adolphus Hart, Definition and Theory in Jurisprudence 7–8 (1953) ("The great anomaly of legal language is our inability to define its crucial words in terms of ordinary factual counterparts.") But see Jacob Israel de Haan, Rechtskundige Significa (1919), cited in Van den Bergh, supra this note, for a twentieth-century Dutch jurist who believed in the perfectibility of legal language.

Saussure rejected the possibility of studying language as an independent entity at all. See Ferdinand De Saussure, Course in General Linguistics 77 (Wade Baskin trans., 1959) Saussure was building on Vico's view of language as a human creation. In a reversal of the more commonly held contemporary view that science provides a higher degree of certainty of knowledge than can be attained in the humanities, the eighteenth-century Vico posited that one gains a deeper understanding of what one creates oneself than is possible to have of the empirically observed outside world. He reasoned that languages, human-created, give rise to superior understanding.

Vico categorized mathematics in the same group as languages, reasoning that, like languages, mathematics were created by humans, rather than empirically observed in the outside world. See Gianbattista Vico, New Science (T.G. Bergin et al. trans. 1948). Vico's view represents a position taken in a still-debated controversy, dating from the time of Plato, over whether mathematics are discovered or invented, with constructivists claiming the latter and formalists the former. For a fascinating discussion of this issue by two eminent French scientists, one a mathematician and the other a biologist, see Changeux & Connes, supra n. 4. See also e.g., Gina Kolata, "Paul Erdos, a Wayfarer at Math's Pinnacle," N.Y.T., September 24, 1996 (taking the view probably more common among mathematicians proper that mathematics are discovered). One of my regrets in life is that my number theorist father died before I could ask him his view. A former colleague of his has suggested that he was a formalist, and my impression is that most mathematicians proper, in contrast to other scientists, are formalists. See A Tribute to Emil Grosswald: Number Theory and Reflected Analysis 5 (Marvin Knopp & Mark Sheingorn, eds. 1990) ("mathematicians operate at a singular disadvantage in the world—they know there is something called 'the truth'"); and Connes, supra this note, at 235 ("my sense of what mathematical research is all about [is] the quest for truth and the inner joy that comes from surrendering oneself to it.")

Hamann, the eighteenth-century philosopher who taught and greatly influenced the German Romanticist Herder on the nature and significance of language, shared Vico's view of mathematics as a human invention. See James C. O'Flaherty, Unity and Language, A Study in the Philosophy of Johann Georg Hamann (1952); and Isaiah Berlin, The Age of Enlightenment: The Eighteenth Century Philosophers 271–75 (1957).

n13. Even this would not be completely true if one credits Freud's theories of an unconscious that separates individuals from an understanding of themselves. See Julia Kristeva, Strangers to Ourselves (Leon Roudiez, trans., 1991) on the subject of the divided self and multiple discourses within individuals.

n14. Willard Van Orman Quine, Word and Object 27 (1960). My definition of Quine's "non-verbal stimulation" here is highly simplified, but is, I hope, sufficient for the purposes of this piece. See Lakoff & Johnson, supra n. 7, at 56 [Metaphors We Live By], for the proposition that not all concepts are understood in terms of other concepts. Some, like the concept "up", derive purely from bodily experience or interaction with the physical world.

n15. I am of the view that understandings across legal cultures diverge somewhat even with respect to concrete "non-verbal stimulus" terms, with understandings capable of approaching, but not reaching, identity. I make no claim, however, that communication of such concepts alone is not generally effective. I nevertheless differ from those comparatists who conclude that, since some (in their view, many) terms are amenable to effective cross-cultural communication, functionalist similarities in different legal systems can be taken at face value. My view is that legal transactions contain few "non-verbal stimulus" terms, that quantity affects quality in this issue, and that the most functionalist of transactions take place in the context of legal systems impregnated with cultural signification, or difference, such that effective legal analysis depends on vigilant sensitivity to differences. For an excellent analysis of divergent French/American conceptions of the judicial opinion, see Wells, "French and American Judicial Opinions," 19 Yale J. Int. L. 81, 101 (1994).

n16. According to George Steiner, true communication lies in a silence beyond lan guage. See George Steiner, Language and Silence, x (1967). For an application of this idea to the function of metaphor, see Curran, supra n. 6 (analyzing the power of meta phoras residing in what is unsaid, in a blank space between the two conflated domains. Both the person who originates the metaphor and the addressee invest their own unique perspectives to achieve conflation). See also Kristeva, supra n. 13, at 16 (referring to "polymorphic mutism" resulting from multiple discourses.) Legal rituals form another, nonverbal means of communication, whose meaning is not grasped even by the actors, resulting in what has been called a "solidarity without consensus." See Garapon, "Que faut-il penser du rite judiciaire?," in Ritual and Semiotics (Jay Knaack & Ralph Lindgren, eds. forthcoming 1997; manuscript on file with the author).

n17. See, e.g., Gordley, "Comparative Legal Research: Its Function in the Development of Harmonized Law," 43 Am. J. Comp. L. 555, 559 (1995) ("One can interpret a code—one can interpret case law—but only because it is not our only source of knowledge of the principles it embodies." Gordley concludes, however, that legal studies can and should be transnational, and that differences in national legal cultures and languages do not preclude identical legal problems from surfacing across borders: "Jurists of different countries may not only be confronting the same problem but seeking the same solution." Id. at 563. Indeed, Gordley's perspective on the need for transnational studies is based on the view that the law often has the same meaning in different countries, with the result that transnational legal studies beget illumination by offering the possibility of deciding which nations' systems are the best.)

But see Charles Taylor, Philosophical Arguments 82 (1995) ("we might meet up with a people to whom we could attribute truth conditions to part of their utterances, and in this way coordinate our actions with theirs and predict them, whereas on a deeper level there remains a profound gap between our conceptual schemes."); and Legrand, supra n. 3, at 120 ("at best, what can be displaced from one jurisdiction to another is, literally a meaningless form of words.")

n18. See Robert Darnton, The Great Cat Massacre and Other Episodes in French Cultural History 7 (1984); Legrand, "Strange Power of Words: Codification Situated," 9 Tul. Eur. & Civil L. Forum 1 (1994); and Legrand, "European Legal Systems Are Not Converging," 45 Int. & Comp. L. Q. 52. 60 (1996) ("The essential key for an appreciation of a legal culture lies in an unraveling of the cognitive structure that characterizes that culture.")

n19. Cover, "Nomos and Narrative," 97 Harv. L. Rev. 4 (1983).

n20. "Vorverständnis," in Hans-Georg Gadamer, Wahrheit und Methode (1960).

n21. Frankenberg, "Critical Comparisons: Rethinking Comparative Law," 26 Harv. Int. L.J. 411, 414 (1990).

n22. "Gemeinsames Erlebnis," in Bernhard Großfeld, Zeichen und Bilder im Recht, 30 NJW 1911, 1915 (1994).

n23. Habermas, "Remarks on Peter Grimm's 'Does Europe need a Constitution?'" 3 Eur. L.J. 303, 305 (1995).

n24. A "*contexte socio-cognitif*" in Legrand, "Le Droit comparé: aujuord'hui et demain," 2 R.I.D.C. 281, 293 (1996). See also Legrand, "Comparative Legal Studies and Commitment to Theory," 58 Modern L. Rev. 262, 265–66 (1995) ("legal practices are very much a reflection of a given culture and of a given legal *mentalité* (in the senses of the internalised culture")).

n25. Quine, supra n. 14, at ix. Quine emphasizes that each person learns language from other people. See id. at 1. Thus, while the discourses of individuals may be unique, they are also interdependent. See also Steiner, supra n. 16, at 233 (Language as the "supreme act of community"); and Ludwig Wittgenstein, Philosophical Investigations 46c–96c (G. Anscombe, ed., 3d ed. 1958) (Words acquire meaning from use and use is a function of the community's intersubjectivities.)

n26. Ainsworth, "Categories and Culture: On the 'Rectification of Names' in Comparative Law," 82 Cornell L. Rev. 19, 25 (1996).

n27. See Ewald, "Comparative Jurisprudence I: What Was It Like to Try a Rat?", 143 U. Pa. L. Rev. 1889 (1995). See also Jürgen Habermas,Between Facts and Norms (William Rehg, trans. 1996). (The importance of balancing the internal perspective with the external one); and Balkin, supra n. 9 (analyzing the philosophy of culture).

n28. For the impressive scholarly breadth of the émigrés, see Zekoll, "Kant and Comparative Law—Some Reflections on a Reform Effort," 70 Tulane L. Rev. 279 (1996). One might add to Zekoll's list Edgar Bodenheimer, Power, Law and Society, esp. The Anthropological Roots of Law 1–61 (1973) (developing an approach of "philosophical anthropology"); and Bodenheimer, "Philosophical Anthropology and the Law," 59 Cal. L. Rev. 653 (1971). One might also refer in this context to such native-born giants in the field as Dawson and Merryman, of the same generation as the émigrés, who, in the words of Lawrence Friedman, were among the "few brave and exceptional souls [to] venture into uncharted territory, [to] attempt something subtler and more difficult [than the comparison of doctrines, rules and procedures; i.e.,] the comparison of legal cultures." Friedman, supra n. 5, at 49. See also Reimann, "German Legal Science," 31 B.C. L. Rev. 837, 844 (The interdisciplinary approach as a tradition in German legal theory.) See Steiner, supra n. 10, at 148, noting these at tributes in refugee professors of comparative literature.

n29. Molière, Le Bourgeois Gentilhomme, act II, scene IV (1670).

n30. See Mattei, "Why the Wind Changed: Intellectual Leadersip in Western Law," 42 Am. J. Comp. L. 195, 218 (1994) ("American academia is becoming more and more turned in upon itself and... the generation of great comparativists that was given to [the U.S.] by the twentieth century tragedy has yet to be replaced.") Steiner describes the analogous "preponderant role" of refugee scholars in comparative literature, noting their polyglot qualities, and, with their deaths, the end of a tradition of reading texts in their original languages. See Steiner, supra n. 10, at 148.

n31. One of the defects of American legal education, in my opinion a serious one, is the failure of law schools to foster sufficient awareness either of connections among the subjects the students study, or of a sense of law as the reflection of a vision not common to all societies. I strongly agree with similar views Alan Watson expresses on this subject in Watson, "Introduction to Law for Second-

Year Law Students?," 46 J. Legal Educ. 430 (1996). On the marginalization of comparative law in United States law schools, see Langbein, "The Influence of Comparative Procedure in the United States," 43 Am. J. Comp. L.545, 546 (1996) For an excellent argument in favor of demarginalizing comparative law, see Reisman, "Designing Law Curricula for a Transnational and Science-Based Civilization," 46 J. Legal Educ. 322 (1996); and Sexton, "The Global Law School Program at New York University," in id. at 329.

(b) *Questions*

1. Why are differences of potential legal interest or significance frequently not perceived?

2. Why is the role of comparison in thinking and analysis frequently not perceived?

3. Is distortion a necessary result of comparison? Does this imply that misperception is intrinsic to perception?

4. Which aspects of communication may be described as unrealizable?

3. *Expanding Our Imagination of Legal Constructs*

In the essay below, William Ewald transports us to sixteenth-century France, a time and a place where animals could be tried in courts of law as defendants in criminal trials.

(a) William Ewald, *Comparative Jusrisprudence (I): What Was It Like to Try a Rat?*
113 University of Pennsylvania Law Review 1889, 1898–1916 (1995)

I. THE RATS OF AUTUN

i.

In 1522 some rats were placed on trial before the ecclesiastical court in Autun. n9 They were charged with a felony: specifically, the crime of having eaten and wantonly destroyed some barley crops in

the jurisdiction. A formal complaint against "some rats of the diocese" was presented to the bishop's vicar, who thereupon cited the
culprits to appear on a day certain, and who appointed a local jurist, Barthélémy Chassenée (whose name is sometimes spelled Chas-
sanée, or Chasseneux, or Chasseneuz), to defend them. Chassenée,
then forty-two, was known for his learning, but not yet famous; the
trial of the rats of Autun was to establish his reputation, and launch
a distinguished career in the law.

When his clients failed to appear in court, Chassenée resorted to
procedural arguments. His first tactic was to invoke the notion of
fair process, and specifically to challenge the original writ for having
failed to give the rats due notice. The defendants, he pointed out,
were dispersed over a large tract of countryside, and lived in many
villages; a single summons was inadequate to notify them all. Moreover, the summons was addressed only to some of the rats of the
diocese; but technically it should have been addressed to them all.

Chassenée was successful in his argument, and the court ordered
a second summons to be read from the pulpit of every local parish
church; this second summons now correctly addressed all the local
rats, without exception. But on the appointed day the rats again
failed to appear. Chassenée now made a second argument. His
clients, he reminded the court, were widely dispersed; they needed
to make preparations for a great migration, and those preparations
would take time. The court once again conceded the reasonableness
of the argument, and granted a further delay in the proceedings.
When the rats a third time failed to appear, Chassenée was ready
with a third argument. The first two arguments had relied on the
idea of procedural fairness; the third treated the rats as a class of
persons who were entitled to equal treatment under the law. He addressed the court at length, and successfully demonstrated that, if a
person is cited to appear at a place to which he cannot come in
safety, he may lawfully refuse to obey the writ. And a journey to
court would entail serious perils for his clients. They were notoriously unpopular in the region; and furthermore they were rightly
afraid of their natural enemies, the cats. Moreover (he pointed out
to the court) the cats could hardly be regarded as neutral in this dispute; for they belonged to the plaintiffs. He accordingly demanded
that the plaintiffs be enjoined by the court, under the threat of severe penalties, to restrain their cats, and prevent them from frighten-
ing his clients. The court again found this argument compelling; but
now the plaintiffs seem to have come to the end of their patience.
They demurred to the motion; the court, unable to settle on the cor-

rect period within which the rats must appear, adjourned on the question *sine die*, and judgment for the rats was granted by default.

This case, and the ingenuity and learning he displayed in defending his clients, established for Chassenée a formidable reputation as a criminal defense attorney. But he was also to contribute influentially to legal scholarship. So far as I am aware, no complete catalogue of his writings exists. But in 1528 he produced two major works. The first, the *Catalogus gloriae mundi*, was an important Renaissance source book on questions of heraldry and aristocratic rank; it was often reprinted. (The catalogues of major American university libraries show holdings of editions from 1546, 1571, and 1579; but the list is not likely to be complete.) The second was his commentary on the customary laws of Burgundy, the *Commentaria super consuetudinibus Burgundiae*. This work, a minor classic of legal literature, n10 was a standard work of reference for French lawyers of the Renaissance. (American libraries hold editions from 1543, 1582, 1616, 1647, 1698, and even 1747; again, the list is probably incomplete.)

Chassenée is said during the 1520s, while he was engaged in his scholarly pursuits, to have continued his practitioner's interest in animals, and to have worked on several cases involving their criminal prosecution. n11 The court records do not appear to have survived; but in 1531 Chassenée himself published a book whose full title is *Consilium primum, quod tractatus jure dici potest, propter multiplicem et reconditam doctrinam, ubi luculenter et accurate tractatur questio illa: De excommunicatione animalium insectorum*—which roughly translates as, *A Treatise on the Excommunication of Insects*. This work, like his other writings, seems to have filled a legal need, for it was reprinted at least twice: in 1581 and again in 1588. n12 This treatise discusses the full range of issues that can have been expected to arise during a trial of "insect animals": the jurisdiction of the lay and ecclesiastical courts, the proper form of the complaint, the issues of notice and of adequate representation by counsel, the procedures to be followed at trial, and the passing and execution of sentences. He cites a remarkable range of obscure and forgotten authors, as well, of course, as various relevant anathemas in the Old and New Testaments—God's cursing of the serpent in the Garden of Eden; the law in Exodus that an ox which gores a man or a woman to death is to be stoned, and its flesh not to be eaten; Jesus's malediction of the barren fig tree of Bethany; the story of the Gadarene swine. He also cites Virgil, Ovid, Cicero, Aristotle, Gregory the Great, the *Institutes* of Justinian, Moses, various patristic theologians, and Pico della Mirandola: the list could easily be extended. He reports numerous examples of successful anathemas pronounced by medieval saints against sparrows, slugs, leeches, eels, and even an orchard. He considers whether animals are to be considered as clergy or as laity. (He concludes that, in general, animals should be presumed to be laity, but that the presumption can be rebutted.) He tries more generally to delimit the exact boundaries separating the jurisdiction of the lay and the ecclesiastical courts; and he draws a careful distinction between punitive prosecutions of animals, and prosecutions that are merely intended to deter future harmful conduct.

Chassenée's fame as an attorney and a scholar continued to grow. No doubt his commentary on the customs of Burgundy contributed more to his legal eminence than did his treatise on the excommunication of insects; but the two works display the same erudition and the same tone of learned seriousness. One might be tempted to suspect Chassenée and his colleagues of an elaborate joke—gargantuan, one might say, in the manner of Rabelais—except that the joke seems to go too far. Chassenée was involved in too many such cases, and his treatise is too laboriously researched, for such an explanation to be credible. He was, after all, an eminent jurist, with many demands upon his time, and in any case the destruction of their barley fields can hardly have seemed a matter for jest to the farmers of Autun.

Chassenée seems to have treated cases involving animals and cases involving humans with equal seriousness, and fortunately we have an instance which leaves no doubt. Near the end of his life, in 1540, Chassenée, whose star had continued to rise, and who was now President of the *Parlement de Provence*, presided over an inquiry into the justice of an order for the extirpation of heresy. n13 Specifically, it was proposed to extirpate some local Waldenses in the villages of Cabrières and Merindol. One of the members of the tribunal, Renaud d'Alleins, suggested that it would be unjust to exterminate the unfortunate heretics without first granting them a hearing, and permitting an advocate to speak on their behalf. After all, had not the President himself insisted upon such a right for the rats of Autun? Did not even animals have the right to assistance of counsel? There can be no doubt of the seriousness with which heresy was regarded: this would not have been an opportune time to remind the President of a joke. Chassenée was persuaded by the arguments of d'Alleins, and obtained from the king a decree that the accused Waldenses should be heard. (This outcome was by no means legally predestined; in fact, Chassenée died in 1541, and the

Waldenses were thereupon exterminated, apparently without obtaining their hearing.)

ii.

It should not be assumed that the courts of Renaissance, when hearing a criminal prosecution against animals, were invariably inclined to decide for the human plaintiffs: not even when the defendants were vermin. In 1545 some wine growers in a village in the district of St. Julien instituted legal proceedings against a species of snout-beetle that infests vineyards. n14 Advocates were duly appointed for the insects. But this first case never came to trial. After consultations with counsel for both sides, the court issued a proclamation, dated 8 May 1546, which observed that God had ordained that the earth should bring forth herbs and fruits, not only for the sustenance of rational human beings, but also for the preservation and support of his lesser creatures, the insects; it would be more fitting for the humans to implore the mercy of heaven, and to seek pardon for their sins, than to proceed rashly against the beetles. The proclamation prescribed prayer, contrition, and the saying of High Mass three times in the vineyards. The insects are reported to have thereupon disappeared from the village.

Forty-one years later, however, in April of 1587, the infestation returned; and this time the animals were actually brought to trial. The court proceedings fill twenty-nine folia, which are preserved in the archives of St. Julien. The legal maneuverings and the arguments about the legal status of animals continued into the summer. In June a compromise was proposed by the advocate for the plaintiffs. A piece of ground, distant from the vineyards, precisely described in its location and dimensions, and well-supplied with plants and herbs, was to be reserved for the use of the beetles in perpetuity. The plaintiffs would retain easements to use the springs on the land, and to cross it without doing detriment to the animals' means of subsistence; they also retained the right to shelter there in time of war, and the right to work the mines of ocher—again, so long as in so doing they did not interfere with the pasture of the animals. (Both parties, it should be observed, agreed that the insects had a legal right to life, and to an adequate share of the earth's bounty: this issue was not in dispute.) n15

The attorneys for the insects did not accept this offer. They argued that the land was in fact barren; moreover, that the mining rights, if exercised by the plaintiffs, would be detrimental to the pasturage of the defendants. The court proceedings continued for many months more. The final outcome of the case is uncertain, the last pages of the court records having subsequently been eaten by some bugs or rats. n16

How frequent were such trials? From the ninth century to the nineteenth, in Western Europe, there are over two hundred well-recorded cases of trials of animals, with the majority falling in the fifteenth, sixteenth, and seventeenth centuries. n17 However, trial records for the medieval period are notoriously spotty, and the actual number must have been much larger. In Elizabethan England such trials were evidently common enough so that Shakespeare could allude to them and expect his audience to understand what he was talking about:

Thy currish spirit
Governed a wolf, who, hanged for human slaughter,
Even from the gallows did his fell soul fleet,
And whilst thou layest in thy unhallowed dam,
Infused itself in thee; for thy desires
Are wolfish, bloody, starved, and ravenous. n18

The animals known to have been placed on trial during this period include: asses, beetles, bloodsuckers, bulls, caterpillars, chickens, cockchafers, cows, dogs, dolphins, eels, field mice, flies, goats, grasshoppers, horses, locusts, mice, moles, pigeons, pigs, rats, serpents, sheep, slugs, snails, termites, weevils, wolves, worms, and miscellaneous vermin. n19

Within this list it is important, as a legal matter, to distinguish wild animals from domestic. As a general rule, the wild animals came within the jurisdiction of the ecclesiastical courts (unless there had been shedding of blood, which could raise complex legal issues), n20 whereas domestic animals came within the jurisdiction of the ordinary criminal courts. n21 The cases I have discussed so far have been cases of vermin, and the primary purpose of the trial was to rid the region of infestation by the threat of anathema or excommunication. In the lay courts, in contrast, the purpose, as a rule, was to punish the animal for its criminal acts: not deterrence, but retribution. n22

An example is the decision of the Law Faculty of Leipzig condemning a milk cow to death for killing a pregnant woman, one Catharina Fritzchen, on 20 July 1621. n23 (German law faculties in the seventeenth century and after, under the institution known as *Aktenversendung*, would often be asked to render judgment in difficult cases.) n24 The cow, condemned as a "monstrous animal" ("*als abschewlich thier*"), was ordered to be transported to a remote, desolate spot, and there executed and buried. n25

Among criminal cases of this sort, there are many instances of pigs being condemned to death for infanticide. n26 A typical specimen is the trial of a sow and her six pigs at Savigny-sur-Etang in 1457; they were charged with murdering and partly devouring an infant. n27 She was found guilty and, like Shakespeare's wolf, was sentenced to death by hanging. Nearly a month later her six pigs were brought to trial. Because of their youth, because their mother had set a bad example, and because the evidence was not sufficient to convict, they were acquitted of the crime.

In cases of bestiality the animal was regularly put to death with the man. It is reported by Cotton Mather that in New Haven, Connecticut, on 6 June 1662, a man named Potter, aged sixty, was hanged with a cow, two heifers, three sheep, and two sows. n28 Animals condemned to death were executed in various ways. Some were burnt at the stake; others merely singed and then strangled before the body was burned. Frequently the animal was buried alive. A dog in Austria was placed in prison for a year; at the end of the seventeenth century a he-goat in Russia was banished to Siberia. n29 Pigs convicted of murder were frequently imprisoned before being executed; they were held in the same prison, and under substantially the same conditions, as human criminals. n30

iii.

These are the phenomena I should like to understand. They perplex and disturb me on a number of different levels. They seem to bespeak a different attitude, on the part of our not-very-remote ancestors, to such matters as: crime, guilt, pain, the person, animals, suffering, truth, death, responsibility, trials, justice, and law. What were they up to, these punishers of animals? What was the point? — I am not sure; and the longer I dwell on the question, the more uneasy and uncertain I become. The issues here are subtle; perhaps we will do best to approach them in stages.

To begin with, I am not satisfied by the explanations, whether medieval or modern, that have been produced for these trials. (Observe that the issue here is the trial, that is the criminal prosecution of the animal by the same formal legal procedures employed for humans: what needs to be explained is not why one would put down a dangerous cow, but why one would first bring the matter to the Law Faculty of Leipzig.)

One explanation of animal punishment was given by the great canon lawyer Gratian in the twelfth century. n31 He held that animals are punished, not because of their guilt (culpa), but so that the hateful act might be forgotten. n32 Another explanation from the sixteenth century takes an opposite approach: animals are punished to inspire in humans horror of the deed, and to keep its memory alive. n33 But neither explanation is satisfactory. The explanation of Gratian raises the question why the animals are to be put on trial and given a gruesome and memorable death rather than simply got rid of and forgotten as quickly as possible. The other explanation raises the question why the particular animal that did the deed is to be punished: if the purpose is to inspire horror in humans, why not kill the animal that will suffer most memorably? And why, indeed, kill just one? Would not a general slaughter be better remembered?

At bottom the problem with both explanations is the same. They sever the nexus between guilt and punishment; Gratian explicitly, and the other approach implicitly. They both assert that (i) injuries caused by animals have nothing to do with culpa, but rather are to be counted among "things that happen"; and, (ii) the purpose of animal punishment is to produce certain psychological effects in humans. But now it becomes difficult to understand why the same reasoning cannot be extended to inanimate objects. Why does one not place on trial the murderous axe, or execute an animal to make vivid to oneself the horror of an avalanche? We have arrived at a reductio ad absurdum for these two lines of justification; or so it would appear.

Another explanation is given by Leibniz in his *Theodicee*. n34 He says that one would be justified in imposing capital punishment on beasts if in so doing one could deter other beasts from evil. (He notes that in Africa lions were crucified to drive away other lions; that wolves were hanged in Germany for the same reason; and that peasants nail birds of prey to the doors of their houses.) Leibniz himself phrases his explanation in the subjunctive mood, and appears sceptical about the deterrent value of capital punishment for animals; but in any case this explanation and his examples would explain only why one kills the beast and displays its body — not the principal issue, which is why one first puts it through the ritual of a formal criminal trial.

Another view of animals was given by an eighteenth-century Jesuit, Guillaume-Hyacinthe Bougeant, in his *Amusement philosophique sur le langage des bestes* of 1739; n35 this work was translated into English in the same year. Bougeant does not directly discuss the animal trials; he was troubled instead by the following problem. n36 As Christianity spreads to pagan regions, and as infants are baptized at birth, the supply of humans available for habitation by devils will constantly diminish. But devils are immortal;

where then are they to dwell? Bougeant answers that the majority of devils are incarnate in the brutes of all kinds. This conclusion he supports by another argument. *Pace* Descartes, animals are not automata, but exhibit thought, knowledge, and feeling; yet they do not have immortal souls, and are not, qua animals, destined either for Heaven or for Hell. But if they are neither persons nor automata, then they must be some third thing; and the only remaining possibility is that they are devils. For this reason, he says, the Christian church has never taken the animals under its protection, or urged kindness towards them. On the contrary, animals have been provided to us by a benevolent God for our use and entertainment. The suffering they endure is part of God's punishment of devils; and when a dog is beaten, or a pig slaughtered, it is the embodied demon that actually suffers. "If it be said that these poor creatures, which we have learned to love and so fondly cherish, are foreordained to eternal torments," he says, I can only adore the decrees of God, but do not hold myself responsible for the terrible sentence; I leave the execution of the dread decision to the sovereign judge and continue to live with my little devils, as I live pleasantly with a multitude of persons, of whom, according to the teachings of our holy religion, the great majority will be damned. n37

Bougeant's views, however, are not medieval: they date from the eighteenth century, more than two centuries after the trial at Autun. His theory that animals exhibit rational thought flew in the face of the received scholastic wisdom; and his theory that animals are in fact demons seems to have been regarded by the Church as highly questionable, if not actually heretical. n38 His arguments are not internally consistent, and in any case do not suffice to explain why, if one knows that an infanticidal pig is a devil condemned to suffer at human hands, one would ever put it through the formal ceremony of a criminal trial.

Some even later writers have seen the purpose of these trials, not in their deterrent effect on other animals, but in their deterrent effect on human beings. n39 But this is a modern explanation; I do not believe it is to be found in the writings of thinkers like Chassenée. Nor does it seem to provide a particularly strong argument for animal trials. Punishing a killer sow seems unlikely to deter a human from infanticide; and when we consider rats or grasshoppers the analogy seems to break down entirely.

Other modern writers have tried to explain these trials by appealing to a theory of personification. They assert that in the Middle Ages domestic animals were regarded as members of the household, and were under certain circumstances even permitted to appear in court as witnesses; from these facts it is inferred that animals were regarded as rational beings, capable of acting as responsible agents. n40 These authors conclude that the purpose of the animal trials and of the subsequent punishment was not so much deterrence as retribution: animals, like humans, are to be held responsible for their actions. But this explanation, too, is problematic. Perhaps it has some limited plausibility for higher mammals, like pigs or dogs; but it hardly seems to work for rats or grasshoppers.

Chassenée, to be sure, thought that the rats of Autun were entitled to notice of their case, and entitled to a hearing. Perhaps—the evidence seems to me ambiguous—he believed that, in some sense, the rats were rational creatures; perhaps, despite his erudition, he shared in a widespread superstition of the common people. But the theologians of the Middle Ages clearly deny to animals the status of rational agents, and Chassenée, at any rate in his more scholarly moods, seems to follow their analysis. Thomas Aquinas, for example, argued that only rational creatures could be the subject of a curse; if God curses an animal (or a place or a thing) the curse must be regarded, not as a curse of the animal per se, but as an indirect way of cursing a rational agent. n41 How, then, asks Thomas, are human curses of animals to be justified? If we regard animals merely as irrational brutes, then the curse would be *odiosum et vanum et per consequens illicitum.* And if we regard the animals as the instruments of God's will, then the human curse would be blasphemous. But a third possibility remains. If the animals are regarded, not as the agents of God, but of Satan, then they may properly be cursed and excommunicated and punished with death: for this is an indirect way of cursing the Devil. (This argument is thus crucially different from the argument of Bougeant, who regarded animals as themselves devils.) Chassenée (who, as I say, may not be entirely consistent in his beliefs on this point) seems to accept this scholastic analysis, and declares in his treatise on the excommunication of insects that the anathema of the Church is not pronounced against the animals in their own person, but through them against Satan.

We have, then, two theories that seek to explain the animal trials in terms of indirect punishment: the theory that animals are punished to intimidate humans, and the theory that they are punished to intimidate Satan. Both theories deny culpa to the animal; both sever the connection between guilt and punishment; both use the suffering of the animal to produce a psychological reaction in the true evildoer. Once again, we seem to be back at our earlier *reductio ad absurdum*. It is not clear why the animal punished and the animal who participated in the crime should be the same; nor why the same reasoning should not apply to inanimate objects. Aquinas and Chassenée propose to prosecute criminally and punish creatures whom they know not to have free will—the guiltless instruments of Satan. But this theory is, if anything, even less comprehensible than the trials it is supposed to explain: we seem to have arrived at the outer limits of intelligibility. For, in its essence, the suggestion of the great philosopher and the erudite lawyer is, it seems, that we should punish, not the cutthroat, but the knife.

iv.

But perhaps we have missed something. Perhaps this outcome would not strike the medievals as a *reductio ad absurdum*, but simply as a further implication of the theory. (It is not a logical mistake.) And if we look in Blackstone, in the chapter dealing with the revenues of the Crown, we find, mixed in with the discussion of rents, profits, ecclesiastical revenues, wine-licenses, shipwrecks, mines, treasure-trove, confiscated property, and escheats of land, a passage in which Blackstone discusses the remnants of the institution known as *deodand*—etymologically, things "given to God." n42 Under this law any personal chattel which was found by a jury of twelve to have immediately caused the death of any reasonable creature was forfeit to the king; the proceeds were to be applied to pious uses and distributed in alms by the high almoner.

Blackstone reports some curious distinctions. (1) No deodand is due if an infant fall from a cart or a horse, so long as the cart or horse is not in motion; but if an adult fall and is killed, the thing is forfeit. (2) If a horse or an ox of its own motion kill an infant or an adult, or if a cart run them over, the thing shall be a deodand. (3) "Where a thing, not in motion, is the occasion of a man's death, that part only which is the immediate cause is forfeited; as if a man be climbing up a wheel, and is killed by falling from it, the wheel alone is a deodand: but, wherever the thing is in motion, not only that part which immediately gives the wound, (as the wheel, which runs over his body) but all things which move with it and help to make the wound more dangerous (as the cart and loading, which increase the pressure of the wheel) are forfeited." (4) No deodands are due for accidents on the high sea, which is not in the jurisdiction of the common law; but if a man fall from a boat in fresh water and is drowned, the ship and its cargo are deodands.

Blackstone has evident difficulty explaining these rules. Point (4) is a simple matter of jurisdiction, and need not detain us. Point (1) he explains in religious terms. The institution of deodand, he conjectures, was originally intended to expiate the souls of the dead, and to pay for masses for those who had died suddenly and in sin. But the child seems, he says, to have been regarded as incapable of actual sin, and therefore to need no propitiatory masses for its soul. (He rejects the explanation of Sir Matthew Hale, that the infant in case (1) receives no deodand because it is unable to take care of itself, pointing out that this fact explains nothing: Hale, too, had evidently struggled to find reason behind these rules.) Points (2) and (3) he explains by "this additional reason, that such misfortunes are in part owning to the negligence of the owner, and therefore he is properly punished by such forfeiture." But the explanation appears to make him uncomfortable. Negligence seems to have played no part in the jury's determination that something was forfeit as a deodand; and Blackstone himself observes that "[i]t matters not whether the owner were concerned in the killing or not; for if a man kills another with my sword, the sword is forfeited as an accursed thing." Indeed, he prefaces his entire discussion of deodands with the remark that this species of forfeiture "arises from the misfortune rather than the crime of the owner."

The entire discussion, measured by Blackstone's usual standard, is remarkably incoherent; he struggles, but is unable to make rational sense of the existing rules. Much as Chassenée might have done, he cites without commentary the Mosaic law about stoning an ox that has killed a human; and he points out that the ancient Athenians would banish from the precincts of the city any object that had caused a man's death by falling on him. n43 But the underlying reasons seem to leave him baffled. He says that the institution of deodand appears to have had its origin in "the blind days of popery," and to reflect the "humane superstition of the founders of the English law." n44 But, he continues, in the present day deodands are for the most part granted out as a royal franchise to the lords of manors, "to the perversion of their original design"; the clear implication is that the institution has outlived its time, and although it did not immediately disappear from English law, it was in fact finally abolished, during the reign of Queen Victoria, in 1846. n45

v.

Armed with this information about deodands, let us return to the animal trials. The problem, recall, was to make sense of the things

Aquinas and Chassenée say about the punishment of animals. We seemed to have arrived at the absurd conclusion that their theory would justify the punishment of inanimate objects; but perhaps to them the conclusion was after all not so absurd.

What light do deodands shed on the original problem? The answer, I think, is some but not very much. In the first place the geographical distribution of the two institutions is not quite right. Deodands seem to have been a creation of English common law, whereas most animal trials took place on the Continent. n46 It is not clear as an historical matter exactly how the institution of deodand arose, or what the primary intellectual sources were: even whether they were pagan or Christian. The Athenians, as Blackstone knew, would put on trial at the Prytaneum three classes of objects: (i) unknown murderers, (ii) animals, and (iii) inanimate objects (stones, beams, pieces of iron) that had caused the death of a man by falling on him. These facts are recorded by Aristotle; Pericles and the famous sophist Protagoras are said to have spent a whole day debating the guilt of an inanimate object. Plato not only mentions such legal proceedings, but evidently approves of them, and in Book IX of the Laws makes provision for their inclusion among the statutes of his ideal commonwealth. n47

But we must beware of drawing too quick analogies between the Athenians, the English, and the French. The purpose of the Athenian practice is perhaps in the end as obscure as the medieval animal trials; but it seems to have been intended to remove an impurity from the community. The original purpose of deodands (if Blackstone's conjecture is correct) was in contrast to provide prayers for the soul of the deceased. And the animal trials seem to have had yet other springs and levers. The connection in Chassenée's mind between animal trials and the cursing of inanimate objects is difficult to fathom. As we saw, he cites two such curses: Jesus's cursing of the barren fig tree of Bethany, and a medieval saint's cursing of a fruit orchard. But Chassenée, like many a lawyer before and since, made a practice of citing whatever precedent lay ready to hand; and these two precedents on inspection seem to have little to do with the institution of deodands, and to shed little light on the trials of animals. The cursing of the figtree was understood allegorically in the Middle Ages as a cursing, not of the tree per se, but of the Jews, whose rituals had brought forth legal foliage but not the fruit of righteousness. And the fruit orchard was cursed, not for any crime it had committed, but because its fruits were keeping the young people of the village from the saint's sermons; once attendance improved, the fruits again began to grow.

It would be an interesting historical exercise to trace these two quite different curses back to their roots, noting the similarities and divergences: one inquiry would involve a study of curses in the ancient world in general, and in ancient Judaism in particular; the other would involve a study of northern European magic and sorcery. In Chassenée's mind the two seem to have blended. But that is not the present point. For neither of these two curses of inanimate objects seems in the relevant respects analogous to the medieval trials of animals. The crucial differences — what sets those trials apart from deodand and from Greek purification rituals — is the element of punishment. The animal trials of course may have been intended (like the Greek rituals) to eradicate a religious taint, and they may also have been intended (like deodands) to give comfort to the soul of the victim. None of this do I deny (although the exact relationship to the Hebrew, Greek, Christian, and northern European rituals seems to me mysterious). But they seem to have had another purpose as well: to condemn and to punish the animals.

vi.

That at least part of the purpose of these trials was punitive can scarcely be in doubt. And it is this element, the punitive element, that I still do not understand. I said before that often the convicted animals were burned at the stake, or buried alive. Sometimes the treatment was even more inhumane, and the animal was tortured before execution. A single example will here suffice for many. In 1386 a murderous sow of Falaises that had torn the face and arms of a child was sentenced first to be mangled and maimed in her head and forelegs; the sow was then dressed in human clothes and slowly hanged in the public square by the town executioner. n48

At this point it is tempting to fall back on the explanation offered by Blackstone, and blame the whole business on the ignorance and the brutality of the medieval world. But this line of reasoning is no less problematic than the others. Chassenée was not in any obvious sense a cruel man (think of his attitude to the Waldenses) and he had read more widely and thought more deeply about the moral standing of animals than has almost any modern attorney. In his thought (and still more in the thought of Thomas Aquinas) the questions about animals are subordinated to a complex moral theology that we may wish to reject as mistaken, but cannot dismiss as primitive.

As for the accusation that these trials were inhumane, it is important to remind ourselves that, after all, the rats of Autun won their case. So too did the snout-beetles of St. Julien. A field was reserved for their use; both parties agreed that even the least of God's creatures has a legal right to live. This attitude contrasts markedly with the modern attitude. One distinguished modern naturalist estimates that, at the present day, as a result of human activity, species of all kinds, but mostly insects, are disappearing at a rate of 27,000 per year — roughly three entire species each hour. n49 We are horrified by the brutality of the animal trials; but it does not take much imagination to see that Chassenée would be equally horrified by our wanton extermination, without trial, of God's creation.

True, he saw animals as creatures who, like humans, could be brought to trial for their deeds and cruelly punished; but from some points of view this must be seen as a sign of moral respect. Where we see in a rat or a pig either useless vermin or a reservoir of animal protein, he saw fellow creatures who enjoyed certain basic rights that can be vindicated at law. Indeed, the entire modern vocabulary of praise and condemnation seems oddly out of place here. We speak of these trials as brutal, and praise the modern world for being more humane; but brutal, in the original sense of the word, is precisely what Chassenée was not. This shift in vocabulary is an important clue. What seems to have happened — what we call being more humane — appears to reflect not so much a greater underlying kindness, or a greater respect for the moral personality of animals, as a greater indifference and a shift in metaphysics. We no longer think of animals as creatures, that is, as created things. We have attained a greater emotional distance from them; we draw a sharper distinction between the animals and ourselves, and are more inclined to view them as automata, as parts of the material world. And when we do accord them some degree of moral respect, there has been an important change in the standard we apply: the higher animals are not to be mistreated, not because they are the handiwork of God, but because they are like us.

At least as a first approximation we can say that Chassenée would have used a different vocabulary than we do: he would have carved up the world differently. He would have divided it, perhaps, into godly and ungodly things. Godly humans and animals appear on one side of his ledger; ungodly humans and animals on the other. This is quite different from the division (which seems to have got its start in the Renaissance) between the brutal and the humane, with all animals falling in one category, and most humans in the other.

A warning may now be in season. I do not wish to suggest that this is the only important difference between ourselves and Chassenée, and the last point about the Renaissance explains why the contrast I have just mentioned can only be a first approximation. The path that leads from Chassenée and the animal trials to ourselves and modern penal science is twisted and at many places hard to follow; perhaps some of the complexity can be brought out by the following observation. It is a common superstition about the Middle Ages that their sensibilities would have been shocked by the discovery of their biological kinship with the animals; but as we have just seen, Chassenée saw humans and animals as being alike God's creatures. He would have acknowledged a kinship, although he did not suppose it to be a biological kinship. It was the humanist philosophers of the Renaissance who first began to talk, in a new way, about the nobility of being human, and to speak of humans as uniquely created in the image and likeness of God. n50 The older view (which of course in Chassenée's day still jostled with the newer one) had counselled humility, resignation, and the insignificance of all things merely human; the newer saw humanity as participating in aspects of the divine. It was the Humanists of the Renaissance and their successors whose sensibilities would have been shocked to learn of their kinship with the apes: the older thinkers would have been surprised, to be sure, but would likely have seen in this kinship only one more deserved chastisement for a fallen human species.

It is important to notice that this difference between the Middle Ages and the Renaissance is not just a matter of new scientific theories, but also involves the discovery of the possibility of new emotional responses to the world—and the loss of some old possibilities. I spoke just now about "sensibilities." The word is important, and should remind us that the differences between ourselves and Chassenée exist, not just at the level of cognition, but also in the very constitution of our moral sentiments. To put the point another way: what separates us from Chassenée—what makes the animal trials both so elusive and so revealing—is not just a shift in a single concept, but in an entire frame of reference. We set out to study these strange legal proceedings of our ancestors; and at every turn we have been brought face-to-face with alien sensibilities, alien metaphysics. And by "metaphysics" here I mean metaphysics in its most full-blooded sense—the subject that addresses such questions as: What is a person? What is an animal? What is the essence of freedom? What is justice? How is reality constituted, and to what ends? To understand Chassenée, it seems, we need to recapture lost images, a forgotten range of experience: an entire way of thinking and feeling about the world.

NOTES

n9. The following account of this incident is taken from two sources. See EDWARD P. EVANS, THE CRIMINAL PROSECUTION AND CAPITAL PUNISHMENT OF ANIMALS, 18–20 (1906); Walter Woodburn Hyde, The Prosecution and Punishment of Animals and Lifeless Things in the Middle Ages and Modern Times, 64 U. Pa. L. Rev. 696, 706–07 (1916).

n10. See HELMUT COING, EUROPÄISCHES PRIVATRECHT, 514 (1985).

n11. See EVANS, supra note 9, at 21.

n12. The following account of the contents of Chassenée's book is taken from EVANS. See id. at 21–33.

n13. The following account of this episode is taken from EVANS. See id. at 19–20.

n14. The following account of the case of the beetles of St. Julien comes from EVANS and HYDE. See id. at 37–49; Hyde, supra note 9, at 705–06.

n15. A similar issue arose in a trial of some grasshoppers in 1565 in the town of Arles in Provence. The counsel for the defense argued that, because the grasshoppers were, in the original sense of the word, creatures, they were justified in eating what they needed to sustain life. The counsel for the plaintiffs cited the cursing of the serpent in the Garden of Eden. In this case, the grasshoppers were condemned, and told to quit the region on pain of anathema. See Hyde, supra note 9, at 707.

n16. See EVANS, supra note 9, at 49.

n17. See HYDE, supra note 9, at 709.

n18. WILLIAM SHAKESPEARE, THE MERCHANT OF VENICE, act 4, sc. 1.

n19. This list is taken from EVANS. See EVANS, supra note 9, at 265–85 (Appendix F). Evans there lists some two-hundred cases, with dates, locations, and species of the defendants. In view of their reputation as witches' familiars, it is perhaps surprising that cats do not appear on the list.

n20. See id. at 31–32.

n21. See id. at 2–3 (crediting the legal historian Karl von Amira with drawing a sharp distinction between animal trials (*Thierprozesse*) and animal punishment (*Thierstrafen*), the former being designed to expel vermin, and the latter to punish animals that were in the service of human beings); HYDE, supra note 9, at 703–04.

n22. I note in passing a curious fact. In medieval villages rabid dogs must have been a common public menace, and must frequently have been put to death.But in the animal trials of which I have read descriptions, dogs are conspicuous by their relative absence. Perhaps dogs were merely regarded as ill, whereas infanticidal pigs were regarded as having a wicked character. The issue here is obviously important, and raises the question of how the Middle Ages distinguished among crime and madness and disease; but I am not aware that this particular problem of the relative absence of dog trials has been investigated.

n23. The decision of the Leipzig Law Faculty is given in EVANS. See EVANS, supra note 9, at 313 (Appendix S).

n24. For a discussion of *Aktenversendung*, see infra text accompanying note 235.

n25. See EVANS, supra note 9, at 313 (Appendix S).

n26. The useful appendices in Evans give many representative samples, in the original languages, of the judicial sentences of condemnation. Eight are of infanticidal pigs. See id.

n27. The following example of the sow of Savigny comes from EVANS. See id. at 298–303.

n28. See Hyde, supra note 9, at 711. To this case can be added the case of Thomas Granger, who was executed in Plymouth in 1642. Granger was a sixteen- or seventeen-year-old servant who confessed to carnal relations with a mare, a cow, two goats, several sheep, two calves, and a turkey. Pursuant to Leviticus 20:15, each of the animals was killed before Granger, who was then himself executed. See 2 RECORDS OF THE COLONY OF PLYMOUTH IN NEW ENGLAND 44 (Nathaniel B. Shurtleff & David Pulsifer eds., Boston, 1855–1861) (12 vols.). I owe this reference to Bruce Mann.

n29. The foregoing examples come from Hyde. See Hyde, supra note 9, at 709–12.

n30. See EVANS, supra note 9, at 142–43 (giving several examples).

n31. See HYDE, supra note 9, at 718.

n32. See id.

n33. See id.

n34. Gottfried Wilhelm Leibniz, ESSAIS DE THÉODICÉE SUR LA BONTÉ DE DIEU, LA LIBERTÉ DE L'HOMME ET L'ORIGINE DU MAL

(Amsterdam, I. Troyel 1710). There is no standard pagination for this work; the passage discussed in the text that follows occurs in @@ 69–70 in the first of the three ESSAIS. In the standard edition of Leibniz's works, it is found at 6 Gottfried Wilhelm Leibniz, Die philosophischen Schriften von Gottfried Wilhelm Leibniz 110 (Hildesheim, Olms Verlas 1960–61) (C.I. Gerhardt ed., 1885).

n35. GUILLAUME-HYACINTHE BOUGEANT, AMUSEMENT PHILOSOPHIQUE SUR LE LANGAGE DES BÊTES (Paris, Chez Gissey 1739).

n36. The following discussion of Bougeant's views is found in EVANS. See EVANS, supra note 9, at 66–67, 80–83.

n37. Id. at83.

n38. The title page of the English translation of his book describes it as "Written originally in French by Father Bougeant, a famous Jesuit; now confined at La Fleche on account of this work." Guillaume-Hyacinthe Bougeant, A Philosophical Amusement upon the Language of Beasts and Birds (1739). I have only seen a card catalogue entry for this translation, which lists the date of the French original as 1737; I have not yet been able to establish the details about the imprisonment at La Fleche. In particular I do not know whether Bougeant was accused of heresy, and, if so, for which of his arguments.

n39. See Hyde, supra note 9, at 718 (citing references to the literature).

n40. Id. at 725–26 (citing references).

n41. The arguments of Aquinas and of Chassenée are summarized, with references, by Hyde. See id. at 716–17.

n42. All the following references to Blackstone's discussion of deodands are found in Book I, Chapter 8 of his Commentaries. William Blackstone, 1 COMMENTARIES ON THE LAWS OF ENGLAND 290–92 (Oxford, Clarendon Press 1765–1769) (4 vols.) (footnotes omitted).

The law of deodands has its origins in the most distant past of English law; the most common medieval deodands were horses, oxen, boats, carts, mill-wheels, and cauldrons. See 2 FREDERICK POLLOCK & FREDERICK W. MAITLAND, THE HISTORY OF ENGLISH LAW BEFORE THE TIME OF EDWARD I, at 473 (1923). Pollock and Maitland observe that "many horses and boats bore the guilt which should have been ascribed to beer." 2 id. at 474 n.4.

n43. According to Pollock and Maitland, who quote Bracton on the point, in older English law the bane, that is the object that caused the death, was itself regarded as the evil-doer. They quote Bracton as saying, "'If a man by misadventure is crushed or drowned, let hue and cry at once be raised; but in such a case there is no need to make pursuit from field to field and vill to vill; for the malefactor has been caught, to wit, the bane.'" 2 Pollock & Maitland, supra note 42, at 473. In this early time, as they point out, the criminal law worked in effect with a theory of strict liability, and its attitude was, "'The thought of man shall not be tried, for the devil himself knoweth not the thought of man.'" 2 id. at 474 (quoting Chief Judge Brian "in words that might well be the motto for the early history of the criminal law").

n44. Pollock and Maitland, in contrast, remark that "[t]he deodand may warn us that in ancient criminal law there was a sacral element which Christianity could not wholly suppress." 2 id.

n45. 2 id. at 473 n.3.

n46. Deodands appear to have spread eastward to Germany from France, with significant modifications on the way. See Hyde, supra note 9, at 730. Hyde also mentions some French cases involving the excommunication of glaciers. See id. at 726.

n47. References to the Athenian practices are furnished by Hyde. See id. at 696–702.

n48. See EVANS, supra note 9, at 16, 140, 287 (Appendix G).

n49. See generally EDWARD O. WILSON, THE DIVERSITY OF LIFE (1992).

n50. The locus classicus for these matters is CHARLES TRINKAUS, IN OUR IMAGE AND LIKENESS: HUMANITY AND DIVINITY IN ITALIAN HUMANIST THOUGHT (1970).

(b) *Questions*

1. How does Professor Ewald's account of the animal trials illustrate the topics discussed in previous sections?

2. What can be inferred from the fact that animal defendants sometimes prevailed in court?

4. *Cultural Contexts of Death and Suicide*

Laws regulate not just life, but also death. The essay below examines underlying differences in society's understandings of life and death at different historical periods and in different parts of the world. Social, cultural and religious beliefs have shaped the legal treatment of suicide, as they continue to do today.

(a) Blanche Grosswald, *The Right to Physician-Assisted Suicide on Demand*[4]

Ethical/Cultural/Religious Attitudes—Western

Not surprisingly, ethical attitudes towards suicide, euthanasia and the right to die vary according to culture, religion, and ethnicity in addition to individual differences.

Ancient Times

Euthanasia and suicide are not new concepts. As far back as ancient Greece and Rome, proponents of euthanasia and physician-assisted suicide were among the majority of their societies in their views. There was no prohibition against suicide (Amundsen, 1997, p. 5). In the fourth century, B.C., Socrates disparaged the position of "lingering death" and commended the god of healing because he would not have tried to cure

> bodies which disease had penetrated through and through..he did not want to lengthen out good-for-nothing lives (Plato, as cited in Tivnan, 1995, p. 97).

Even Plato, Pythagoras, and Aristotle who in general were against suicide, believing it to be a cowardly way of escaping one's obligations to society, did support it for people enduring "great suffering" (Plato, as cited in Rachels, 1986, p. 8; Alvarez, 1971). Zeno, founder of Stoicism, committed suicide due to an unbearable physical pain (Zeno, as cited in Emanuel, 1994, p. 793). The Stoics considered suicide "the most reasonable and desirable of all ways out" (Alvarez, 1971). Seneca, another Stoic philosopher, supported the

---

4. This text is an excerpt from a longer work of the same title.

right to suicide for any reason (Seneca, as cited in Rachels, 1986). Epictetus concurred:

> If the room is smoky, if only moderately, I will stay; if there is too much smoke, I will go (Epictetus, as cited in Rachels, 1986).

Pliny the Younger described a common situation in Rome during the first century in which a suffering man questions doctors as to the terminality of his illness, with the intention of ending his life if he indeed has a fatal disease. For these ancient Greeks and Romans, the distinction between passive or active euthanasia, mercy killing, or physician-assisted suicide was not germane. If someone were terminally ill and in pain, it was considered acceptable to have even non-physicians assist in a voluntary suicide. For example, while Pythagoras, Plato, and Aristotle considered suicide cowardly, they were in favor of suicide and assisting suicide for cases of terminal illness and pain (Rachels, 1986, p. 8).

Western Ethical/Philosophical Concepts

Natural Rights

The concept of natural rights is one that John Locke, among others, supported. It refers to the idea that society has an obligation to protect certain rights, such as the right to life or the right not to be killed. This is distinguished from euthanasia with the person's consent. Because rights over one's own body are usually included as "natural" rights, euthanasia for the terminally and painfully ill is supported by proponents of natural rights theory. However, they do not necessarily extend these rights to include support for suicide in general.

Personhood

Respect for "persons" is Kant's perspective on ethics. He defined "persons" as moral agents, i.e., those beings with a capacity for making moral judgments. Although he was in favor of self-determination for "persons" in many cases, he opposed euthanasia on the basis of the point of view that the lives of "persons" are valuable and therefore must be continued. His respect for self-determination is described by his "Formula of Autonomy" (Kant, 1785, p. 98) in which he both explains that humanity, composed of rationality and autonomy, is infinitely valuable and that, therefore, a human life must never be ended.

The contemporary controversy stemming from Kant's definition of "person" is the debate about what constitutes a "zoological" versus a "biological" life. The set of people who are "alive" is not equivalent to the set who "have life." Having a biography, possessing psychological attributes, the capacity to have hopes, fears, and ideas are part of the definition of having "bios." This is distinguished from simply being alive or having "zoe." Medical terms that have acquired legal definitions in today's society such as "brain-dead" and "vegetative state" refer to the idea that someone may be alive without, however, being capable of having a life (Kushner, 1995). This differentiation in turn leads to the debate about "quality of life," which lives society should preserve, and which ones are not deemed worthy of saving.

A contemporary scholar associated with the American Enterprise Institute, Leon Kass, interprets the early writings by Hobbes and Locke on natural rights and by Kant on personhood as distinctly advocating against the philosophical right to physician-assisted suicide (Kass, 1993, pp. 34–40). From Hobbes and Locke, Kass extrapolates that "the right to life is a matter of nature, not will" (Kass, p. 38). The possible change in will from a desire for life towards a desire for death did not, according to Kass, give humans the new right to die.

Many health care professionals view their primary role as one of saving lives rather than saving people from pain. Many people subscribe to the moral value that life is good and death is bad. Moreover, death is to be avoided not only because of effects on survivors, but because of the damage to the person her/himself.

Natural Law

An argument heard frequently against the right to commit suicide has to do with the idea that suicide is somehow "unnatural." It goes against the natural order, the self-preservation instinct, and, for religious people, it violates God's will. Kant believed that suicide was wrong in part because it violated nature. If a person committed suicide in order to relieve her or his own suffering, that would mean that acting out of "self-love" would lead to self-destruction. Moreover, Kant went on to claim, a logical contradiction followed from the idea that self-love could lead both to life preservation and to ending life. Kant found this not compatible with "a system of nature" (Kant, 1785, p. 89). However, this argument of Kant's does not appear sound. As Cosculluela points out (1995, p. 34), Kant is making a strange assumption that everything in nature must have a purpose and that self-love in particular must have one. There is no reason to support the assumption. Moreover, it is quite possible that under certain circumstances, self-love would lead to life preservation, while, under different circumstances, self-love would lead to suicide. When enjoying life, self-love would result in the tendency to preserve life. When enduring mental or physical pain, self-love could follow a self-destructive path. If, by definition, suicide is a form of self-destruction, then a suicide committed in order to relieve oneself of unbearable suffering is one committed from self-love.

Cultural/Religious Attitudes — Non-Western

Hoefler and Kamoie (1994) pooled together information on cultural differences in right-to-die attitudes from a variety of sources. In comparing non-western to western attitudes regarding death, euthanasia, and suicide, their thesis is that Westerners, but especially Americans, fear death more than non-Westerners. When examining non-Western cultures, the authors cite evidence that African attitudes towards death are influenced by their communalistic rather than individualistic values; the Islamic belief of death as merely one stage of life; the Japanese worship of certain types of suicide; and the Buddhist positive outlooks on "mujo" or impermanence of life stages as well as their belief in reincarnation (Hoefler and Kamoie, 1994, pp. 22–23). The impact of these attitudes is that euthanasia and suicide are more acceptable in these non-Western cultures than in the U.S. While a value placed on the common good rather than the individual might appear to lead to an anti-suicide position, the lesser emphasis on the individual is associated with less of a negative attitude towards any individual's death. In the U.S. and the West in general, the individualist mentality corresponds to a fear and denial of death.

Africa

Wiredu (1990, as cited in Hoefler and Kamoie, 1994, p. 22) explains that the Akan clan of Ghana rely on a family's decision when right-to-die issues arise for an individual. Economic and individualistic pressures of Western countries do not play an equivalent role in Akan culture.

Islam

According to M. Adil Al Aseer (as cited in Hoefler and Kamoie, 1994, p. 22), although Islam forbids suicide, Islamic courts have made judgments on right-to-die cases on a cost-benefits basis, from the point of view of the family, the doctors, and the society as a whole.

India

During the Vedic age (1500–1000 B.C.) of India, suicide was allowed for religious reasons. The Vedas considered human sacrifice to the Gods the highest form of sacrifice.

The Upanishads, writings during the 600–300 B.C. period, held a more mixed attitude towards suicide. While some condemned the practice, others allowed it under specific circumstances, such as at certain sacred locations like the "confluence of rivers" or by people suffering from terminal illnesses (Venkoba Rao, 1975, p. 232). The Bhagavad-Gita condemns both self-mutilation and suicide.

Hindu philosophy affects the way Indian people feel about suicide. The key concepts of "karma," meaning cosmic justice and reincarnation, maintain that people are re-born into a state of life whose attributes depend on how one behaved the last time around. Part of this philosophy includes the cheerful acceptance of death. Nevertheless, suicide is still condemned by Hinduism except in special cases.

An important exception is "sati," the practice of throwing oneself onto the funeral pyre of a husband by his widow. This ancient custom changed gradually throughout India's history. During the Vedic era, the widow was only expected to lie down for a few minutes on the pyre before cremation. Eventually, the custom turned into a practice more like murder with many women being thrown into the fire against their will. Finally , an Indian social worker, Raja Ram Mohan Roy, protested against "sati." It was made illegal in 1892.

Contemporary religions of India are Hinduism, Jain, and Buddhism, all of which affect the attitude towards suicide held by Indians today. Suicide by fasting or "sallekhana" is sanctioned by the Jain religion. This was also advocated by Gandhi as a political tool.

Some of the common motives for suicide in India include wishing to marry against parental consent; fear on the part of unmarried women of being a burden to one's parents; and infertility. While these are often sources of unhappiness for Westerners as well, they are not as likely to be cited as reasons for suicide attempts (Venkoba Rao, 1975). One also could interpret this type of suicide as being a form of societally sanctioned euthanasia in which deviants die.

Taiwan

Contemporary society in Taiwan has both Buddhist and Confucianist influences. Buddhists believe that human life is difficult and that people who commit suicide do so because they cannot handle the stress of life. While Buddhism thus contains an attitude of compassion towards suicidal people, at the same time it maintains that their souls never can reincarnate. Confucianism (like Hinduism) condemns suicides except for those done out of loyalty to family or country. Suicide is regarded as immoral because it involves destroying one's body, a gift from one's parents (Rin, 1975).

Japan

Japan has a reputation for not only permitting suicide, but for promoting it in situations which many Americans might have trouble understanding. In addition to the "accepted" areas of U.S. right-to-die controversial cases—the terminally ill, the severely disabled, and those in severe physical pain—Japanese people commit suicide (usually in the form of hara-kiri) for reasons such as failing a school entrance exam, bringing dishonor to one's family, and in ancient times, disloyalty to the Emperor. Kato (as cited in Hoefler and Kamoie, 1994, p. 22) lends support to Japan's image regarding suicide, explaining it in part as a result of the Buddhist tradition in Japan. Because Buddhism does not view death as unusual or a state to be avoided, euthanasia or suicide has not been prohibited. Moreover, the idea of "death with dignity" or "sonshi" has enjoyed high regard in traditional Japanese culture, as compared to its recent place in U.S. society (Shapiro, as cited in Hoefler and Kamoie, 1994, p. 23).

Domino and Takahashi compared Japanese to U.S. attitudes towards suicide (Cited in Takahashi, 1997). The Japanese surveyed were more likely than Americans to believe that suicide is not abnormal and, indeed, that it is an acceptable practice. The Americans were more likely to consider suicide a result or symptom of a mental health problem. There is a word in Japanese "boshi-shinju" which means mother-children murder-suicide. The implication of having such a word in one's language is that the Japanese view this act as a form of extended suicide, rather than as murder-suicide. Japanese consider children to be part of their mother. Society is not only not critical of this type of suicide, but a mother who kills just herself receives more criticism than if she also had killed her children. This is in stark contrast to the U.S. perspective if one considers the example of the reaction to Susan Smith, the mother in South Carolina who claimed to have killed her children because she was planning to commit suicide. Another Japanese word, "inseki-jisatsu," refers to a suicide to take responsibility. This may result from a failure at work and in very recent times also form a layoff from a job (Takahashi, 1997, pp. 138–143).

A recent study on "do not resuscitate" orders ("DNR") of the terminally ill at a Japanese University hospital showed that Japanese patients had significantly less input into the decision to effect a DNR order than patients in other countries (5 % compared to 14–41 %). The results were interpreted to mean that there is no agreement in Japan concerning informing a patient about her/his medical condition, especially if it is terminal. In the particular research under consideration, only 35 % of the subjects who died of cancer even knew their own diagnosis. Obviously, without the necessary information, people cannot participate in euthanasia or right-to-die decision-making. Nevertheless, when surveyed, more than 60 % of the Japanese population claimed to wish to be informed of terminal diagnoses (Fukaura et al., 1995).

NOTES

Alvarez, A. (1971). *The savage God: A study of suicide*. New York: Random House.

Amundsen, D.W. (1997). The significance of inaccurate history in legal considerations of physician-assisted suicide. In R.F. Weir (Ed.). *Physician-assisted suicide*, Chapter 1, pp. 3–32. Medical Ethics Series. Smith, D.H. and Veatch, R.M. (Series Eds.). Bloomington, IN: Indiana University Press.

Cosculluela, V. (1995). *The ethics of suicide*. Garland Studies in Applied Ethics, Vol. 4. Garland Reference Library of Social Science, Vol. 1033. New York: Garland.

Emanuel, E.J. (1994). The history of euthanasia debates in the United States and Britain. *Annals of Internal Medicine*, 121, 793–802.

Domino, George; Takahashi, Yoshitomo., Attitudes Toward Suicide in Japanese and American Medical Students. Suicide and Life-Threatening Behavior v21, n4 345–359.

Fukaura, A., Tazawa, H., Nakajima, H., & Adachi, M. (1995). Do-Not-Resuscitate orders at a teaching hospital in Japan. *New England Journal of Medicine*, 333, 805–808.

Hoefler, J.A. & Kamoie, B.E. (1994). Policy Restraint and the Cultural Context of Death. Chapter 2. In *Deathright: Culture, Medicine, Politics, and the Right to Die*, pp. 21–42. Boulder, CO: Westview Press.

Kant, I. (1947).*Groundwork of the Metaphysic of Morals*. (H.J. Paton, Trans.). London: Hutchinson's University Library. (Original work published in 1785).

Kass, L. R. (1993). Is there a Right to Die? *Hastings Center Report*, 34–43.

Kushner, T. (Spring, 1995). Lecture Notes. *Medical Ethics*. Health and Medical Sciences. University of California, Berkeley, CA.

Rachels, J. (1986). *The End of Life: Euthanasia and Morality*. Oxford: Oxford University Press.

Rin, H. (1975). Suicide in Taiwan. In N.L. Farberow. (Ed.). (1975). *Suicide in Different Cultures*, Chapter 16, pp. 239–254. Baltimore, MD: University Park Press.

Takahashi, Yoshitomo (1997). Culture and Suicide: from a Japanese Psychiatrist's Perspective.(Suicide: Individual, Cultural, International Perspectives) Suicide and Life-Threatening Behavior v27, :137–145

Tivnan, E. (1995). *The moral Imagination: Confronting the Ethical Issues of our Day*. New York: Simon & Schuster.

Venkoba Rao, A. (1975). "suicide in India." In N.L. Farberow. (Ed.). (1975). *Suicide in Different Cultures*, Chapter 15, pp. 231–238. Baltimore, MD: University Park Press.

(b) *Question*

1. What underlying outlooks does Professor Grosswald view as being compatible with the greater non-western tolerance of suicide?

V. Ought *versus* Is: A Challenge to Comparative Legal Analysis

1. *Introduction*

Lon Fuller argues against the view that we should analyze law in terms of what is, rather than what should be. In the passage below, he examines positivism, the view that law is what the state says it is, in terms of whether such a perspective can claim moral legitimacy.

Professor Fuller's discussion also fits into a larger framework of determinism inasmuch as his rendition of positivism raises a specter of confusing what is with what must be.

2. *The Struggle to Define Law*

(a) Lon Fuller, The Law in Quest of Itself, 18–41
(The Foundation Press, 1940; reprinted by AMS Press, 1978)

Savigny and his followers assumed that there could be such a thing as a "bad rule of law," that is, a rule of law that did not truly express the spirit of the people. This "bad law" must, however, acquire its validity as law from some principle foreign to the theory of the historical school itself. And if such a principle exists, then the notion that the law emanates from the spirit of the people turns out to express, not a criterion of the law that is, but a particular kind of natural-law standard for the law that ought to be, and the historical school loses all pretensions to being "positivistic" in the sense in which I am using the word here.

Our historical survey of positivism could be made more intelligible if we were able to say definitely of each positivist what objective he was pursuing, and what it was that led him to prefer the route of positivism to that of natural law. Unfortunately this is not possible with the later positivists, for by the time we reach them what Vaihinger called "the law of the preponderance of means to end" has begun to operate, and men have lost sight of the purposes of positivism in manipulating its apparatus. When we go back to the man who may be said to be the father of legal positivism, however, this difficulty is not present. With Thomas Hobbes[5] there was no uncertainty or ambiguity about the object which he pursued in constructing his theory. It has been said without paradox that he founded legal positivism on a natural-law basis. His argument ran something as follows. If we look over the objectives, material and spiritual, which men may seek to attain, we see at once that one of these objectives — that of peace and order — is a precondition of all the others, and hence is entitled to priority over them. Without a certain degree of peace and order, art, literature, science — even the enjoy-

---

5. Among Hobbes' writings the work most relevant to our discussion is, of course, LEVIATHAN. (Subsequent references will be to the pagination of Smith's Edition, Oxford Univ. Press, 1909.) See also THE ELEMENTS OF LAW (ed. Tönnies, Cambridge, 1928) and *A Dialogue of the Common Laws,* in 6 WORKS (Molesworth, 1840) 3–160.

Although historical treatment of the doctrine of sovereignty — something I make no pretension of offering here — would of course have to include a study of Bodin. I have felt it possible to leave him out of account in these lectures, partly because his positivism was apparently , of a very "impure" variety, being more heavily tinctured with natural law than Hobbes'; and also because his work has not appreciably influenced later writers on legal (as distinguished from political) subjects. See on Bodin, MCILWAIN, CONSTITUTIONALISM AND THE CHANGING WORLD (1939) 40–55, and *passim*; and SABINE, A HISTORY OF POLITICAL THEORY (1937) 399 *et seq.* The assertion of Gurvitch *[Droit naturel ou droit positif intuitif?* (1933) 3 ARCHIVES DE PHILOSOPHIE DU DROIT ET DE SOCIOLOGIE JURIDIQUE 55, 59] that Hobbes' view was anticipated by Protagoras seems unjustified by the scanty references to Protagoras' philosophy contained in Plato and Diogenes Laertius. To be sure, the issue of convention *versus* reason is a theme which recurs frequently in Greek philosophy. But what is lacking in Greek thought is the notion of any organ set up to act as a final arbiter of convention. So far as the underlying spirit of Hobbes' philosophy is concerned, Sabine suggests that among the Greeks the Epicureans were probably closest to him.

ment of the grosser physical pleasures, are all impossible, and the life of man is "solitary, poore, nasty, brutish, and short."

How are we to obtain this minimum of peace and order, however, in view of the fact that the interests of men tend inevitably to come in conflict, so that in a natural state men are at war with one another? We cannot bring about this condition of peace and order by reasoning with men. Even assuming that men would always follow right reason if it were given, many of the questions of mine and thine which separate men are not immediately susceptible of solution by reasoning. What is therefore needed is some earthly authority which shall have final power to settle these questions, which shall act as a kind of artificial reason to take the place of natural reason in solving these questions. This earthly power we shall call the Sovereign, and the rules it lays down for the settlement of disputes we shall call Law. This Sovereign should in establishing the law follow the precepts of natural reason as far as these will carry it. Unfortunately, however, there is no possible way of guaranteeing that it will do this. Though reason itself dictates many things about the content of the law, there is no way of drawing a hard and fast line between those things which can be settled by reason and those which must be settled by fiat. Therefore to permit men to pass judgment on the commands of the Sovereign in the light of reason would be to invite revolution and disorder. Men ought accordingly to obey even the unreasonable and unjust commands of the Sovereign, for the evils which flow from obedience are less than those which flow from disobedience. Not only must we follow the commands of the Sovereign, but we must refrain from embroidering them with our own conceits. For if it is true that without the sovereign Power "every man would be wolf to another," the first step toward making every man a wolf to his fellow is to allow him to interpret the law as he sees fit.

It will be noted that this view—so simple in its essence that it can hardly be called a "theory"—in no way denies that human reason ought to play an important role in shaping the law. It touches only the question of the sanction which this "ought" should carry. Hobbes himself sets up an elaborate series of principles of natural reason which the Sovereign ought to follow, and his enumeration is in fact more detailed than that of most modern jurists who champion the notion of natural law.[6] It is on this basis that Stammler is

6. See especially Chapters 14, 15, 21, 27, and 30 of LEVIATHAN.

justified in classifying him, without explanation or apology, along with Pufendorf and Grotius as an exponent of natural law, distinguishing him from the second of these authors chiefly by his assumption that man's fundamental nature is antisocial.[7]

It will also be noted that Hobbes' conception of sovereignty is not overburdened with distinctions and definitions. Where Hobbes becomes complicated and sophistical is not in expounding the notion of sovereignty, but in justifying it; not on the positivistic side of his theory, but on the natural-law side. His attempts to show that the sovereign power results from a grant running from the people to the sovereign, and that this grant must in its very nature be irrevocable, are remarkable for their laborious ingenuity but for little else; certainly not for their power to induce conviction. We shall not concern ourselves with them here, for they have had no influence on the later history of legal positivism. The later positivists have not attempted to prove the need of a sovereign power; they have assumed it. The problem which caused Hobbes so much pain they have solved by ignoring it.

On the other hand, of the numerous difficulties which have vexed the later exponents of the imperative theory, only one is discussed at any length by Hobbes. If we define law as the command of the sovereign, what shall we say of the law laid down by the judges? Being subject to the King, or the Protector, they are certainly not sovereigns in their own right, and if they were, of course the unity and effectiveness of the legal order would be destroyed. It would be natural to regard them as agents of the sovereign, were it not for the fact that their decisions customarily purport to rest not upon the sovereign will, but upon independent sources, chiefly custom and reason. If the judges are agents, they are agents who habitually talk as if they were principals. This difficulty Hobbes solved by a very simple expedient of method which has been accepted by his followers ever since, and which consists essentially in disregarding the judges' talk. The judge may not think he is an agent of the sovereign, but he is, since the sovereign adopts the judge's will as his own.[8] What the sovereign permits, he impliedly commands. The principle of agency that the act ratified must have been done by one who purported to act as agent seems not to apply in the higher field of positivistic jurisprudence.

---

7. Rechts-Und Staatstheorien der Neuzeit (2d ed. 1925) 15. See also Del Vecchio, Lezioni di Filosofia del Diritto (3d ed. 1936) 65; Bergbohm, Jurisprudenz und Rechtsphilosophie (1892) 164; Robertson, Hobbes (1886) 142.

8. Leviathan 213 [143].

It has not infrequently been intimated that the high value which Hobbes put on peace and order resulted from some streak of cowardice in his character, aggravated perhaps by the disordered times in which he lived. This interpretation stands in strange contrast to Hobbes' own combative nature, so strongly revealed in the polemical writings which usurped a large portion of his intellectual energies. If his view had its origin in his personality, I should prefer to think that it was a reaction against what he regarded as a disruptive and wasteful impulse in his own nature. The man who prides himself on his willingness to do battle, "the man who loves a good fight," is often the victim of a modesty which was foreign to Hobbes. One who feels himself incapable of anything more productive than fighting will naturally experience no sense of the tragic waste involved in dispute. Hobbes was not of this class. He truly expressed his own motives, I think, when he wrote at the end of his *Leviathan* that he hoped that he had in that work sufficiently disposed of the Artificial Body called the State so that he might return to his "interrupted speculation of Bodies Natural." He sought peace for creative work in a world which was filled with combative impulses, including his own. Yet this fact offers us no basis for condemning his view as "escapist." To the extent that his theory expressed an aspect of his own personality, it at the same time expressed a need of civilized men everywhere.

When we pass down to Hobbes' successors, from among whom we may select Austin and Somló as outstanding, we discover that "the imperative theory of law" has undergone an enormous change.[9] It is now imbedded in such a maze of distinctions and defi-

---

9. See AUSTIN, LECTURES ON JURISPRUDENCE (4th ed. 1879), and SOMLÓ, JURISTISCHE GRUNDLEHRE (2d ed. 1927). (Somló's book, with its extensive bibliographical apparatus, offers an excellent means of access to the whole literature of positivism.)

Of course it is impossible for me to attempt to deal adequately here with the whole school of "analytical jurisprudence." See Pound, *The Progress of the Law, Analytical Jurisprudence, 1914–1927* (1927) 41 HARV. L. REV. 174; Pound, *Fifty Years of Jurisprudence* (1937–1938) 50 HARV. L. REV. 557, 51 HARV. L. REV. 444, 777; Kocourek, *The Century of Analytic Jurisprudence since John Austin*, printed in 2 LAW, A CENTURY OF PROGRESS (pub. by New York Univ. Press, 1937) 195.

One of the most curious books in the history of legal positivism is BERGBOHM, JURISPRUDENZ UND RECHTSPHILOSOPHIE (1892). In this work Bergbohm attempted to show that all of the supposedly positivistic theories of his day were in fact heavily infected with natural-law elements. In a projected second volume he planned to lay down definite criteria of positivism which would remedy this situation and completely exclude natural law from legal thinking. The second volume never appeared.

nitions that it is difficult at times to recognize it as deriving from Hobbes' simple and common-sense view. These complications in the theory have, I think, arisen in two different ways.

In the first place, they in part reflect an increased complexity in the structure of the state. The problem which plagued Austin, how to locate the sovereign power in a government of checks and balances and distributed powers, caused Hobbes no concern. He was able to assume, without too much violence to the facts, that the sovereign power in England would be lodged in a single man, either a King or a Protector. As government became more complex, the concept of sovereign power as a unifying force became more difficult to maintain, since it could no longer derive its unity from its seat in a single human being. An increase in the complexity of the governmental structure to which it related was bound to produce complications in the theory itself.

In the second place—and this is, to my mind, the less obvious but more important factor—what Hobbes viewed as an ethical desideratum, to be achieved with as close an approximation as human affairs permit, was viewed by his successors as something existing independently of the objects it was intended to accomplish. There is, to be sure, the question just what kind of "reality" the later positivists attributed to their sovereign. But whether they regarded it as a datum of nature, or only as a kind of postulated reality with an inner logic of its own like the plot of a play, their sovereign was something to be described, not, as with Hobbes, a program to be carried out. In thus cutting the theory of sovereignty loose from its natural-law roots they paved the way for the subtle and futile discussions which surround later positivist theories.

In attempting a summary of the theory of sovereignty in the form it assumed with the analytical jurists, I shall not undertake a comparison of the views of different authors. What is necessary for our present purposes is a survey of the kinds of questions which have caused embarrassment to Hobbes' successors, and a brief indication of the methods employed in answering them. The similarity of these questions to certain problems of theology is readily apparent, and will be referred to later. I shall try to state the position of the analytical jurists as sympathetically as possible. If their solutions often seem verbal and formal, we must remember that this is not because they preferred solutions of that kind, but because that was the only sort of solution open to them in view of the questions they thought had to be answered. We must judge their achievements in the light of the objectives they sought.

As I have already pointed out, one problem, which we may call that of the *Little Sovereign*, had already been disposed of by Hobbes. This was solved by saying that the man who looked like a Little Sovereign—the judge, let us say—was, in the eyes of analytical jurisprudence, only an agent of the Big Sovereign.[10] That this construction of the judge's position was contrary to his own understanding of it was quite immaterial, because if his own understanding were adopted it would destroy the unity of the legal order, which is, in turn, an essential assumption if we are to retain any criterion of the law *that is*. Nor are all of those who influence the growth of the law to be admitted even to the rank of Vice-Sovereign. Text-writers and professors, for example, help to shape the law, but they are not accorded the position of agents of the sovereign. They are merely persons whose opinions may influence the sovereign or its agents.[11] That a prediction of the way this influence will work may rest on a more secure factual basis than a similar prediction concerning a statute is, of course, immaterial. We are interested not in the forces which actually shape men's conduct, but in a legal construction which reduces those forces to juristic coherence.

The question, how is the sovereign power to be located in a given society? was answered so satisfactorily by Austin that the later positivists have generally accepted his answer without cavil. That answer was, in brief, to say that the sovereign is that person or group of persons which society is in the habit of obeying.[12] It is clear that this conception rests the legal order ultimately on custom, since the sovereign is, under this view, merely the beneficiary of a custom of obedience, and the security of his position will depend upon the strength of the custom supporting it.[13] It is equally obvious that in

---

10. AUSTIN, *op. cit.* 104; SOMLÓ, *op. cit.* §106.

11. AUSTIN, *op. cit.*, *Lecture XXX*; SOMLÓ, *op. cit.* §106, p. 359; HOBBES, LEVIATHAN 212 [143].

12. AUSTIN, *op. cit.* 226 *et seq.*; SOMLÓ, *op. cit.* §29.

13. Del Vecchio goes a step further and penetrates not only behind "the sovereign," but also behind the "habit of obedience" which makes the sovereign. He argues that the most enduring reality in the whole complex of factors which create "the law" lies in human reason, since whether a given system of law will receive general acceptance—whether it will engender the requisite habit of obedience—depends ultimately on the appeal it makes to human reason. *Il Problema delle Fonti del Diritto positivo* (1934) 14 RIVISTA INTERNAZIONALE DI FILOSOFIA DEL DIRITTO 184.

Cf., "Turn now to that faction of the positivistic party which has all law take its origin exclusively in and through the state, and which regards the

reality the role of custom is not limited to determining the sovereign power, but that the content of the law itself, and the allocation of power, among the sovereign's agents, are also in large part determined by custom. It is furthermore clear that it may be custom rather than the sovereign power which furnishes the basic stability of a society, for as Portalis observed, "L'expérience prouve que les hommes changent plus facilement de domination que de lois."[14] For Austin and his followers, however, these effects of custom are mere factual realities without jurisprudential significance. In the eyes of analytical jurisprudence custom acts *ex proprio vigore* only in establishing the sovereign; any other effects it may have exist only by the tolerance of the sovereign and are therefore by implication in accordance with his assumed commands.

It follows from this that if occasionally certain commands of the sovereign are ignored, if particular laws are in practice disobeyed with impunity, this does not destroy their character as laws.[15] If it did, our test for the law *that is* would be lost. We could no longer inquire whether the particular rule was commanded, expressly or impliedly, by the sovereign, but would have to inquire instead to what degree the particular rule managed to get itself realized in the affairs of men. Since this is obviously a matter of degree, we would have forfeited our test of the law *that is* and would have opened a great door to contamination from the law that merely ought to be.

The degree to which particular laws are enforced and obeyed is immaterial unless disobedience reaches a point which compels us to say that the sovereign which issues these laws no longer enjoys the obedience of the bulk of society in the generality of cases. In that event we are either in a condition of anarchy or—and this is more usual—new sovereign power has emerged.[16] It has been said that nature makes no leaps; it may be said of Austin's school that it never moves except by leaping. It recognizes big revolutions, but not

---

statute as the only true form of law. Now you seem to be on solid ground; here at least a man knows where he stands. You are wrong! Pursue your inquiry a little farther, go beyond the notion of the state, and you will find yourself right where you started. All the things against whose arrogated law-giving power you were once so earnestly warned are back on the scene again: 'the nature of man', 'the natural right of the stronger'—the same 'peaceful order' founded on 'reason.' . . . you've spoiled it all by asking too many questions." BERGBOHM, JURISPRUDENZ UND RECHTSPILOSOPHIE (1892) 116–117.

14. *Discours Préliminaire*, in 1 LOCRÉ, LA LÉGISLATION DE LA FRANCE (1827) 244, 251.

15. SOMLÓ, *op. cit.* §35.

16. AUSTIN, *op. cit.* 230–240; SOMLÓ, *op. cit.* §§31–32, §§39–40, §95.

little ones. It recognizes changes in an abstract thing called the sovereign, but not in the fabric of men's daily lives. It is clear why this should be so. Basically the quest of positivism is for some test which will designate plainly the law *that is* and distinguish it from the law that is merely becoming or merely ought to be. This test is found by Austin and his school in the concept of the sovereign. This concept cannot possibly perform its function unless it has permanence and unity, unless it can absorb and survive the little revolutions which go on all the time.[17]

More embarrassing for the positivists than the points just discussed is a set of questions which arise out of what we may call *The Problem* of *the Inconsiderate Sovereign*. The concept of sovereignty is intended to introduce unity into the legal order and make positivism possible. If our actual sovereign is what we may call a considerate sovereign he will refrain from doing anything which would impair his usefulness for analytical jurisprudence. He will, first of all, treat himself as legally omnipotent, because if there are any legal limitations on his power we shall have to call in some undesignated third party to act as an arbiter over these limitations and the door will be left ajar for an invasion from the juristic underworld of natural law. For the same reason, our considerate sovereign will not issue contradictory commands, for if he does we might be tempted to take into account considerations of what ought to be in deciding which of his commands to follow. Again, if he is especially considerate, he will see to it that his commands cover the whole field of possible dispute, for if there are gaps in the law, who is to fill the gaps, and how?

But suppose our actual sovereign turns out to be inconsiderate of the demands of legal positivism?[18] Suppose, as a first example, he declares that his powers are legally limited? Analytical jurisprudence has two ways of dealing with this infraction of juristic principle. If there is someone in sight who can take over his functions, the recalcitrant sovereign is simply demoted.[19] If the legislature decrees that

---

17. "Stünde hinter ihnen [i.e., these minor changes] nicht auch ein relativ fester Kern, so könnte ja von einem Rechte und einem Staate überhaupt nicht gesprochen werden." SOMLÓ, *op. cit.* p. 313.

18. The difficulties of the task of forcing the fact of government into the jurisprudential mold of sovereignty seem at times to become oppressive for Somló. In one place he declares, "Es ist keine geringe Aufgabe, die Sprüche des Rechtsmachtsorakels zu entziffern, zu deuten und in die klare Form eines Sysems zu giessen." *Op. cit.* p. 17.

19. See the references in notes 12 and 16 *supra*.

its laws once passed can be changed only by a two-thirds vote of the populace, then we may declare that "the real sovereign power" is located in two-thirds of the people, and the legislature is only an agent of this higher power. If there is no other power capable of taking over the duties of our original sovereign, the situation is more embarrassing. There is then left only one step, and that a bold one. That is to declare that these self-imposed limitations are invalid. Our sovereign is so powerful that he lacks the power to limit his own power.[20]

As to contradictory commands, we shall resolve all doubts in favor of assuming that our sovereign is conscious of his duties to jurisprudence, and that what appears as a contradiction is only apparently so. We are, naturally, cut off from this course if the sovereign himself declares that his commands are or may be contradictory. In that case we are forced again to say that the sovereign is simply wrong; in the eyes of analytical jurisprudence he cannot contradict himself.[21] This should not be mistaken for a *legal* limit on his powers; his powers remain legally without limit but are subject only to certain jurisprudential restrictions. Neither should these limits on the sovereign's powers be regarded as deriving from natural law, for natural law has to do with the Good Life, while these restrictions

---

20. AUSTIN, *op. cit., Lecture VI*, espc. at 254, 264, 270–298. Somló considers that the sovereign can promise as well as command, but the obligation imposed by the sovereign's promise rests entirely on what Austin called "positive morality"; "legally" the sovereign may withdraw his promise at any time. *Op. cit.* §94 and §104.
" . . . the Bodin-Hobbes-Austin proposition, that sovereign power is incapable of legal limitation, while often denied, is an inescapable proposition of logical truth. There can be nothing more ultimate than ultimateness." Kocourek, *op. cit. supra*, note 9, 200. *Cf.*, " . . . the right to make binding obligations is a competence attaching to sovereignty." Hughes, C.J., in Perry v. United States, 294 U.S. 330, 353 (1935).
21. "The proposition that all the expressions of the highest legal power must be construed into a consistent system of legal rules follows from the nature of law itself. It is therefore inescapable. It cannot be affected by possible provisions of the law to the effect that the expressions of the sovereign must not be interpreted, or that each expression of the legislator must be considered in isolation. It cannot even be abrogated by an express rule that contradictions of the legislator are not to be construed away." SOMLÓ, *op. cit.* 383. See also HOHFELD, FUNDAMENTAL LEGAL CONCEPTIONS (1923) 136. Though Kelsen dispenses with the notion of the sovereign, he also postulates the impossibility of conflicts inside a single legal order. REINE RECHTSLEHRE (1934) 84–89. He explains that if such conflicts were permitted, "dann wäre es um die Einheit der Rechtsordnung geschehen." One might add that legal positivism would also be visited with the same extinction.

proceed from certain ethically indifferent requirements of juristic theory.

The problem of gaps in the law is perhaps the most difficult of all. Legal positivism certainly has an interest in sealing up as many gaps as it can in the system of positive law, for every gap represents a possible point of entry for natural law and ethics. One solution for this problem is to say that there really are no gaps in the law because what the sovereign has not forbidden he impliedly permits. Accordingly, if the plaintiff cannot bring his case within the existing system of constraints set up by the sovereign, we must enter judgment for the defendant, and this judgment is in effect directed by an implied command of the sovereign. This is the theory of the plenitude of the existing legal order in its most extreme and repressive form.[22] Generally legal positivism, not wishing to be accused of blocking the growth of judge-made law, has solved the problem of gaps in the law in a more abstract and less inhibitive manner. Though there may be no rule in advance for the particular case, there is a judicial machinery ready to handle the case. The judge who decides the case is the authorized agent of the sovereign; his commands are the commands of the sovereign. Accordingly, there really are no gaps in the law, since the unprovided-for case is actually provided for; the sovereign decrees in advance that in the case of "novel impression" the rule to be applied shall be that which his agent, the judge, considers proper.[23] It is again immaterial that this is not the way the judge himself views the thing. That he refuses to decide the case because there is in his opinion "no law" governing it, does not establish the existence of a gap in the law, because from the standpoint of analytical jurisprudence a decision for the defen-

---

22. See BERGBOHM, JURISPRUDENZ UND RECHTSPHILOSOPHIE (1892) 373; and the writers discussed in SOMLÓ, *op. cit.* §115. Hobbes' view was that in the absence of more explicit direction the sovereign should be considered as impliedly ordering the judge to decide the case according to the "law of nature." LEVIATHAN 209 [141].

23. SOMLÓ, *op. cit.* § 117. In solving the problem of what he calls "technical gaps" in the law, Kelsen arrives at substantially the same solution, though of course without introducing the notion of sovereignty. REINE RECHTSLEHRE (1934) §§40–41. Both Somló and Kelsen consider that the supposed problem of "gaps in the law" has been largely imagined into existence, for political reasons, by the adherents of natural law. Somló likens these jurists to the hungry fellow in Mark Twain's story who ate a shoe and, on being asked which part he liked best, replied, "The holes." What the partisans of the law of nature like best about the positive law, according to Somló, is its holes, and they naturally tend to exaggerate their extent and importance. SOMLÓ, *op. cit.* p. 410.

dant is as much a decision of law as a decision for the plaintiff.[24] The judge makes law even when he states that he is refusing to make it, and the law which he thus makes is by adoption that of the sovereign. This solution may seem a trifle verbal, but at least it maintains the principle of positivism formally intact.

Analytical jurisprudence approaches theology most closely perhaps in dealing with the interrelations of its own trinity, which consists of the Law, the State, and the Sovereign. Are these three things, or three aspects of the same thing? Is the State the personification of the Law, or is the Law an instrument of the State? Is the State something set up by the Sovereign, or is the Sovereign merely the personification of the power of the State? I shall not attempt to discuss these finer points of political theory here. The fact that they have been solemnly disputed by intelligent men in the twentieth century is evidence enough, however, of the danger of attempting to deal with conceptual entities without reference to the ends they are intended to serve, and is another exemplification of Nietzsche's trenchant dictum that the commonest stupidity consists in forgetting what one is trying to do.

(b) *Questions*

1. In what way does Professor Fuller view Hobbes' positivism as founded on natural law?

2. What distinguishes positivism from natural law?

3. How would the role of judges be envisaged by a positivist? By a natural-law adherent?

---

24. KELSEN, REINE RECHTSLEHRE (1934) §40; Goble, *Affirmative and Negative Legal Relations* (1922) 4 ILL. L. Q. 94, 98; (1919) 28 YALE L.J. 387, 391 (a Case Comment by Professor Cook). For critical comment on this view see Pound, *Fifty-Years of Jurisprudence* (1937) 50 HARV. L. REV. 557, 574, n.81; and Fuller, *Legal Fictions* (1931) 25 ILL. L. REV. 887, 892 n.208.

VI. The Globalized Future

1. *Introduction*

The following article illustrates the kinds of cultural clashes that arise when international laws are drafted by and for peoples from different legal cultures.

2. *The Encounter of Legal Cultures in Negotiating a Multilateral Treaty*

(a) E. Allan Farnsworth, *A Common Lawyer's View of His Civilian Colleagues*
57 Louisiana Law Review 227 (1996)

I. Introduction

In recent years, the difficulty of conversations between cultures has become a fashionable subject of discourse. If you have seen, perhaps even read, a popular book entitled "Men Are From Mars, Women Are From Venus," you may recall that it bears the alternate title, "A Practical Guide for Improving Communication and Getting What You Want in Your Relationships." n1 The relationships meant are, of course, those with the other culture—the opposite sex. But you may also want to bridge other cultural gaps than those engendered by gender, for instance the gap between common lawyers and their civilian colleagues. It is this gap that I will address.

To begin with, I must confess that, unlike many of my distinguished predecessors in the Tucker Lecture series—such as René

David, Paul André Crépeau, and André Tunc (to mention just a few from the French tradition)—I am neither a civilian nor a card-carrying comparatist. I have never taught a comparative law course, never belonged to an organization of comparatists, and never reveled at one of the congresses held by comparatists in exotic parts of the world. So I come to my topic as a simple common lawyer. I have, however, some familiarity with the problems of communication between our two legal cultures as a result of having negotiated and drafted with civilians in two important endeavors.

The first came during the decade of the 1970s, when I represented the United States at the United Nations Commission on International Trade Law (UNCITRAL) in the negotiation and drafting that culminated in the diplomatic conference in Vienna that produced the United Nations (Vienna) Convention on Contracts for the International Sale of Goods. The Convention is a multilateral treaty to which the United States and over forty other countries are now parties. It governs contracts for the international sale of goods much as Article 2 of the Uniform Commercial Code governs domestic sales.

The second opportunity came during the 1980s and early 1990s when, for roughly a decade, I was a member of the group at the International (Rome) Institute for the Unification of Private Law (UNIDROIT) that recently produced the UNIDROIT Principles of International Commercial Contracts. The Principles, in contrast to the Convention, are not a treaty but merely a set of rules that the parties to a contract are free to incorporate by agreement. They are designed to be suitable for contracts for services as well as for sales.

It would be a mistake to suppose that the only cultural differences that needed to be resolved in UNCITRAL and UNIDROIT were those between common lawyers and civilians. There were differences between the industrialized countries and the developing countries, and there were differences, at the times in question, between the free market countries and the socialist countries. I will not go into these, however, confining my remarks to the differences between those of us who are common lawyers and our civilian colleagues.

I can assure those of you who are students that the course in comparative law I had in law school gave me at least a passing familiarity with the civil law that was indispensable in coping with those differences. n2 Those of you who study law here in Louisiana have a unique opportunity to acquire more than a passing familiarity with the civil law, and you never know when it will come in handy. When the distinguished jurist James Kent went on the bench in New York in the early nineteenth century, he described how his familiarity with the civil law came in handy: "I made much use of the Corpus Juris, and as the judges (Livingston excepted) knew nothing of French or civil law, I had immense advantage over them." n3

I will speak mainly of the differences and peculiarities that I have found—on both sides—when common lawyers meet with civilian colleagues. But just as there are differences among civilians, so too there are differences among common lawyers. So, I begin with a few observations about the peculiarities of American common lawyers that distinguish them from the English, the Australians, the Ghanaians, and others of our breed.

II. American Peculiarities

In one way we Americans are closer than our common law brethren to our civilian colleagues, for we Americans come with our own codifications, something quite unknown in other common law systems. Just as civilians look first to the provisions of their codes and only then to the cases that have applied those provisions, we Americans do the same with our Uniform Commercial Code. In this we are unique in the common law world. Jurists the world over are familiar with our Uniform Commercial Code. And while my civilian colleagues at the UNCITRAL and UNIDROIT meetings had little interest in decisions of common law courts, whether from America or England or elsewhere, their attitude toward our Code was quite different. Indeed, the Uniform Commercial Code has been one of our best exports. n4 When UNCITRAL met in New York, my civilian colleagues occasionally commissioned me to buy them copies of the Code at my law school's bookstore. The delegate from the Soviet Union had translated the Code into Russian. It is not surprising that one can find traces of the Code scattered throughout the Vienna Convention and the UNIDROIT Principles.

As you probably know, the Uniform Commercial Code has a particular civil law influence because of its principal moving force, Karl Llewellyn (of whom Chancellor Hawkland spoke in his Tucker Lecture last year). As a teenager, Llewellyn had been sent to a Gymnasium in Mecklenburg, Germany, in the thought that he might find more profit there than in high school at home in Brooklyn. When the first World War broke out, Llewellyn's affection for Germany took him from a Paris café to the front with the German army. He was wounded, hospitalized, and awarded the Iron Cross. After the war, he twice taught at Leipzig as a visiting professor and maintained a lifelong interest in civil law in general and in German law in particular. n5 It is, therefore, no coincidence that a centerpiece of the Code is the concept of good faith—much as the analogous concept of *Treu und Glauben* is a centerpiece of the German Civil Code. Were it not for this kinship of the Code with its European cousins, it might, I assume, have been more difficult in 1993 for Louisiana to have achieved a compromise between Louisiana law and the Code in your new civil code provisions on sale of goods.

In addition to our Code, we Americans have our Restatement. And though you have been taught that the authority of a Restatement is not that of legislation, the fact that the form of the Restatement resembles that of a code is not lost on our civil law colleagues. I turn now from differences among common lawyers to the main subject at hand—differences between common lawyers and their civilian colleagues. I will treat differences of approach, style, terminology, and substance. First then, a difference of approach.

III. A Difference of Approach

Common lawyers and their civilian colleagues have traditionally taken very different views as to the role of legislation. Here is the view of Portalis, reflected in the French civil code: "The function of the law *loi* is to fix, in broad outline, the general maxims of justice droit, to establish principles rich in suggestiveness consequences, and not to descend into the details." n6 A corollary of this view that a code should contain general principles is that a code contains all of the required general principles—it is a seamless body of law with no gaps. To simplify everything is an undertaking the value of which we would all have to admit. To anticipate everything is a goal impossible of achievement. Grant Gilmore, architect of Article 9 of our Uniform Commercial Code, described a civilian code as

> a legislative enactment which entirely pre-empts the field and which is assumed to carry within it the answers to all possible questions: thus when a court comes to a gap or an unforeseen situation, its duty is to find, by extrapolation and analogy, a solution consistent with the policy of the codifying law....n7

It is in this vein that Article 4 of your Louisiana Civil Code provides, "when no rule for a particular situation can be derived from legislation or custom, the court is bound to proceed according to equity. To decide equitably, resort is made to justice, reason, and prevailing usages." n8 By way of contrast, a common lawyer's code is still, to some extent, viewed as a collection of diverse statutes enacted against the backdrop of the common law. This view is reflected in a tradition of narrow construction of statutes by common law courts that would startle our civilian colleagues. Certainly no civilian would have authored the remark of a learned English observer in 1882 that some of the rules of statutory interpretation in his country's courts "cannot well be accounted for except on the theory that Parliament generally changes the law for the worse, and that the business of the judge is to keep the mischief of its interference within the narrowest possible bounds." n9 I should interject here, since many of my quotations are from across the Atlantic, that English drafting—though assumed by many civilians to be identical to ours—differs from American drafting, and I much prefer the latter. But, both differ markedly from the civilian view. Section 1-103 of the Commercial Code makes it clear that this code is not, as Gilmore put it, "a legislative enactment which entirely pre-empts the field and which is assumed to carry within it the answers to all possible questions...." n10 That section provides: "Unless displaced by the particular provisions of this Act, the principles of law and equity...shall supplement its provisions." n11 Observe that the reference is not, as in the Louisiana code, to "justice" and "reason," but to "law and equity," which means to a common lawyer the body of case law—from law courts and equity courts—that antedated the Code. The Code states what I call the "Swiss cheese theory" of code interpretation: Regard the Code as a piece of Swiss cheese with all its holes, and if, when you search for a solution to your case, you find a hole in the Code, look through it to the backdrop of case law. Here is a major difference in approach between ourselves and the civilians.

How did we common lawyers and the civilians work out this difference in the Vienna Convention? The more numerous civilians had some success. What they got, in article 7(2), was this: "Questions concerning matters governed by this Convention which are not expressly settled in it are to be settled in conformity with the general principles on which it is based." n12 Portalis would have approved this invitation to reason by analogy. But we common lawyers also had some success. What we got, in the balance of article 7(2) was this: "In the absence of such principles, [matters not expressly settled by the Convention are to be settled] in conformity with the law applicable by virtue of the rules of private international law." n13 Here is a recognition of the Swiss cheese theory: Look at the Convention as a piece of Swiss cheese, and, if you see a hole in the Convention, look through it to the backdrop of the law that would otherwise apply under choice of law rules. This concession to the common lawyers was all the more remarkable because the predecessor of the Vienna Convention—the less widely adopted Uniform Law on the International Sale of Goods—had said exactly the opposite. It had explicitly rejected the Swiss cheese theory by excluding rules of private international law "for the purposes of the application of the present Law." n14

From a difference of approach, I turn to a difference of style.

IV. A Difference of Style

Anyone who compares the writing styles of jurists, whether in drafting legislation, opinions, contracts, or whatnot, cannot fail to notice that common lawyers are more prolix than their civilian counterparts and that American jurists are the most prolix of all. The poet John Donne—who knew English lawyers from his education at Lincoln's Inn—thus caricatured those lawyers nearly four centuries ago:

> In parchments then, large as his fields, he draws
> Assurances, bigge as gloss'd civill laws,
> So huge that men (in our times forwardnesse)
> Are Fathers of the Church for writing lesse. n15

The propensity of common lawyers to write on and on has elicited a variety of plausible explanations, n16 and I have one of my own to add—one that may appeal to the student reader. It is that the lecture method practiced for centuries by our civilian colleagues in their great law schools, such as Bologna and Paris, reassures the student: all will be well if you will only trust the application of our great general principles. This is not just the case for civilian lawyers. According to the French mathematician Jules Henri Poincaré, "on the Continent mechanics is taught always more or less as a deductive and a priori science." n17 But instruction in the common law, particularly by the Socratic method practiced in this country, proceeds on a very different assumption. To again quote Poincaré: "The English teach mechanics as an experimental science." n18 In common law, faculties experiment with our cases, real and hypothetical, and discuss everything that can possibly go wrong with a transaction. Far from reassuring our students, we produce in them a profound, if healthy neurosis, which can only be alleviated when later called upon to draft by resorting to detail in the hope of covering all variations of their model. No wonder that common lawyers draw, as John Donne put it, "Assurances...So huge that men...Are Fathers of the Church for writing lesse." n19

Everything we common lawyers write tends to the longer than what our civilian colleagues write, but this is particularly true of statutes. Civilians are comfortable with legislation, reflecting the view of Portalis, that it should only "fix, in broad outline, the general maxims" and not "descend into the details." n20 Not so the common lawyer. For in spite of the current flood of legislation in all common law countries, common lawyers are still more comfortable with cases. Most would subscribe to the confession of Lord Coke centuries ago that, "if it be common law, I should be ashamed if I could not give you a ready answer; but if it be statute law, I should be equally ashamed if I answered you immediately." n21 The common lawyer's mistrust of legislation was put to good use by W. S. Gilbert in Iolanthe:

> And while the House of Peers withholds its legislative hand,
> And noble statesmen do not itch
> To interfere with matters which
> They do not understand,
> As bright will shine Great Britain's rays
> As in King George's glorious days. n22

Against this mistrust, common lawyers who draft legislation use the defense of prolixity. So it is that the Uniform Commercial Code takes about 220 words to state the seller's implied obligations as to quality of goods while the Vienna Convention takes only 160 (and would probably have taken less if common lawyers had not had their hand in it).

For a graphic demonstration of the difference, take the matter of definitions. Definitions are largely alien to the civilian tradition. You have only a few avowed definitions in your Louisiana Civil Code. (I say "avowed" definitions because it is not uncommon for civilian codes to conceal definitions as substantive rules—as your Louisiana Civil Code does for such terms as "confirmation" and "ratification," which appear in the guise of substantive rules. n23)

In contrast, to make sure that unfriendly common law judges will not misinterpret legislation, legislatures in common law countries provide judges with a profusion of definitions. Article 2 of our Code begins with a list of three dozen definitions peculiar to the sale of goods, in addition to the nearly fifty general definitions in Article 1, for a total of over eighty. You may recall Lord Mildew's dictum in *Bluff v. Father Gray*: "If Parliament does not mean what it says, it must say so." n24 By definitions, the common lawyer attempts to say so.

How did the common lawyers and the civilians work out this difference in the Vienna Convention? Here the civilians—more numerous than the common lawyers—prevailed. True to the civilian tradition, the Convention lacks avowed definitions—though there are a few concealed ones, since provisions such as that of article 25 on "fundamental breach" are plainly definitional.

From this difference of style, I turn to a difference of terminology.

V. A Difference of Terminology

Discussions at UNCITRAL went on in six official languages, those at UNIDROIT in two working languages. The problem of translation sometimes exposed differences in terminology. Thus, you will find that the English text of the UNIDROIT Principles uses the term "good faith and fair dealing," while the equally authentic French text says only "*bonne foi*"—on the ground that "fair dealing" is implicit in the French term for good faith. And those from the French tradition will be amused to find that the UNIDROIT Principles render *force majeure* the same way in English, while those from the English tradition will enjoy finding that the Principles render "hardship" the same way in French.

Aside from such questions of translation, the legal jargon of common lawyers differs from that of our civilian colleagues. Every common lawyer knows that in a sale of goods it is the buyer who is the "debtor" and the seller who is the "creditor," because it is the buyer who owes the price to the seller. And every civilian knows that in such a transaction it is the seller who is commonly called the "debtor" and the buyer the "creditor," because it is the seller who has the duty to render the characteristic performance, delivery of the goods. This difference was resolved in the UNIDROIT Principles when I joined the Working Groupby deleting the words "debtor" and "creditor" from the original drafts, prepared by civilians, and replacing them with "obligor" and "obligee."

Then there is the matter of Latin maxims. Common lawyers now enter the profession with no more Latin than *expressio unius and ejusdem generis*—if that. Our civilian colleagues, however, at least those from Europe, cherish such singular maxims as *suum cuique tribuere* (to render to everyone his own). Nothing can be done about this in polite conversation. But in drafting both UNCITRAL and UNIDROIT have accepted the principle that Latin words are not to be used. While the older and "Eurocentric" Uniform Law on the International Sale of Goods spoke of "ipso facto avoidance," its successor, the Vienna Convention, has nothing but English words.

I now turn from approach and style to substance.

VI. Some Differences of Substance

What differences of substance divided the common lawyers and their civilian colleagues at UNCITRAL and UNIDROIT? Though there were many, I shall confine myself to three that arose at both UNCITRAL and UNIDROIT and that were particularly troublesome: the duty of good faith performance, the availability of specific performance, and the enforceability of penalty clauses.

First, we consider good faith. The concept of good faith plays a major role in civilian contract law. The most remarkable example is Article 242 of the German Civil Code, which requires parties to observe *Treu und Glauben*—a few words that have spawned a vast outpouring of caselaw. To the civilian mind, good faith is a broad reaching concept that covers far more territory than the comparable provision of Uniform Commercial Code 1-203, which requires good faith in the performance of contracts. n25 English law, at the opposite extreme from the civilians, adamantly refuses to recognize any such duty of good faith whatsoever. The common lawyers at UNCITRAL, uneasy with the vague and expansive civilian concept of good faith performance, adamantly refused to accept a provision in the Vienna Convention requiring good faith performance; the civilians sternly insisted on the inclusion of such a provision. Which camp prevailed? Consider article 7(2): "In the interpretation of this Convention, regard is to be had to...the need to promote...good faith in international trade." n26 What should you make of this? The common lawyer will tell you that since it speaks only to the interpretation of the Convention, it was a harmless compromise that cannot possibly impose a duty of good faith on the contracting parties. But some civilians suggest that it is a Trojan horse that will enable a civilian judge or arbitrator to impose a duty of good faith on a contracting party. Not a very happy compromise between the two views. What do the UNIDROIT Principles say? No compromise there. Under article 1.7, each party "must act in accordance with good faith and fair dealing...." n27 A clear victory for the civilians.

Second, we turn to specific performance. As most of you know, courts in civilian legal systems routinely grant specific performance by ordering parties to perform their contracts. But courts in common law systems, for reasons that are largely historical, regard specific performance as an "extraordinary" remedy, to be granted only when an award of damages would not be "adequate." n28 (I might add here that we Americans sometimes rationalize the denial of specific performance on the ground that this permits a party to a contract to commit an "efficient breach," but that concept of law and economics is one that not only does not travel well, but that struck most of my civilian colleagues as bordering on the immoral.) How, then, was this fundamental difference resolved in the Vienna Convention?

Look first at article 46, which provides that a "buyer may require performance by the seller of his obligations...." n29 Here it seems that the civilians carried the day. But now look at article 28, which provides that if a party "is entitled to require performance of...the other party, a court is not bound to enter a judgement for specific performance unless the court would do so under its own law in respect of similar contracts of sale."n30 This was a victory for the common lawyers, but think of what it means. Suppose that an importer of some standard commodity such as spices has a choice between suing an exporter in London or in Paris. If suit is in London, article 28 will qualify article 46, and the English court will not be required to grant specific performance. It would not do so under English law for a contract to sell spices, so it is not required to do so under the Convention. But if suit is in Paris, article 28 does not affect the French court. Since it would routinely grant specific performance under French law, the importer can get specific performance under article 46. The result under this awkward compromise therefore turns on which forum—London or Paris—the plaintiff chooses, a less than satisfactory result for a convention intended to make law uniform.

How do the UNIDROIT Principles resolve this difference? Article 7.2.2 begins by providing that "where a party who owes an obligation other than one to pay money does not perform, the other party may require performance." n31 The Principles have no provision comparable to the awkward compromise of article 28 of the Vienna Convention. Instead, under an exception to the general rule of article 7.2.2, a party that "may reasonably obtain performance from another source" n32 cannot require performance, which brings the rule close to the traditional common law position.

Finally, we come to penalty clauses. Another profound difference between these two legal cultures relates to the validity of penalty clauses. Civilians generally find nothing objectionable in provisions imposing penalties for breach. Courts in common law countries, however—again for reasons that are largely historical—refuse to enforce provisions imposing penalties (unless, of course, they are cleverly disguised as "liquidated damages"). How did the Vienna Convention resolve this difference? It did not resolve it at all, because the subject was considered "too hot to handle." The Convention, therefore, has no provision on penalties. When the Convention was finished, UNCITRAL created another Working Group, which attempted to draft a special convention on this touchy subject. But it was indeed "too hot." While UNCITRAL did produce its Uniform Rules on Contract Clauses for an Agreed Sum Due Upon Failure of Performance, they were buried with a pious Resolution of the General Assembly in 1983 that admonishes courts to give "serious consideration" to the Rules and "where appropriate, implement them." No country has, and it is unlikely that any country ever will.

What about penalties under the UNIDROIT Principles? Surprisingly, article 7.4.13 says: "Where the contract provides that a party who does not perform is to pay a specified sum to the aggrieved party for...non-performance, the aggrieved party is entitled to that sum irrespective of its actual harm." n33 A court or arbitrator may, however, reduce the sum to a reasonable amount if it is "grossly excessive." What was too hot for UNCITRAL to handle was easily dispatched by the drafters of the Principles, and in accord with the civilian view.

VII. A Difference and an Explanation

Here, then, are three examples dealing with good faith, specific performance, and penalties. In the case of good faith UNCITRAL achieved an ambiguous compromise. In the case of specific performance UNCITRAL settled for a clear but non-uniform compromise, and in the case of penalties UNCITRAL was unable to do anything effective. And yet as to all three, the UNIDROIT Principles have clear solutions—not compromises—the first and third generally in accord with the civilian view and the second close to the common law position. (I should note in passing that while I have had time to discuss only these three particularly troublesome examples, the solutions to the three that I have discussed reflect what I think was the dominance of the civilian view at UNIDROIT.) What can be the reasons for this difference and the apparently greater success of the UNIDROIT Principles in resolving differences between common lawyers and civilians? Here are two.

First, the Vienna Convention is a multilateral treaty—along with a constitution, the highest form of legislation. The UNIDROIT Principles are not legislation at all, but merely terms that the parties can incorporate if they so choose. This is a particularly compelling explanation in the case of specific performance. Under the proposed revision of Article 2 of our Uniform Commercial Code, a court will be permitted to grant specific performance "if the parties have expressly agreed to that remedy." n34 And if the parties have incorporated the Principles, they have so agreed. But this is not the only explanation.

Second, the United Nations is a politicized organization, and, at the time in question, UNCITRAL had within it clusters of industrialized, socialist, and developing countries. In United Nations commissions such as UNCITRAL, delegates represent their governments, procedure is formal, and interventions are translated into the official languages, which had become six in number by the time of the diplomatic conference in Vienna. UNCITRAL, on the contrary, is less politicized—in its origins largely Eurocentric. In its Working Groups members do not serve as government representatives, procedure is often informal, and interventions are often not translated into the other of the two working languages.

For these reasons it proved to be easier for both groups, common lawyers and civilians, to make concessions at UNIDROIT than at UNCITRAL. Although—indeed, perhaps because—the results at UNIDROIT were less dramatic than those at UNCITRAL, the ability to work together and reach effective compromises were greater. If common lawyers are from, say, Saturn and civilians are from, say, Jupiter, A Practical Guide for Improving Communication between the two would do well to look to the model of UNIDROIT.

NOTES

n1. John Gray, Men Are From Mars, Women Are From Venus (1992).

n2. See E. Allan Farnsworth, Looking in from Outside your Garden: Another View of Comparative Law, in The Responsiveness of Legal Systems to Foreign Influences 413, 422 (Swiss Institute of Comparative law 1992).

n3. Peter Stein, The Attraction of the Civil Law in Post-Revolutionary America, 52 Va. L. Rev. 403, 408 (1966).

n4. This is so though it has been said by a distinguished comparatist that "any comparative appraisal of the Uniform Commercial Code is rendered difficult by its lack of basic similarity with the typical European or Latin-American commercial codes." Rudolf B. Schlesinger, The Uniform Commercial Code in the Light of Comparative Law, in 1 Study of the Uniform Commercial Code 57, 74 (N.Y. Law Revision Comm'n Leg. Doc. No. 65(A) (1955)).

n5. He also spent brief periods before the war at the universities of Lausanne and Paris. See William Twining, Karl Llewellyn and the Realist Movement, ch. 6 and Appendix A (1985). See also James Whitman, Commercial Law and the American Volk: A Note on Llewellyn's German Sources for the Uniform Commercial Code, 97 Yale L.J. 156 (1987).

n6. Jean Étienne Marie Portalis et al., Discours préliminaire (1827), as quoted in Arthur T. von Mehren & James R. Gordley, The Civil Law System 54 (1977).

n7. Grant Gilmore, Legal Realism: Its Cause and Cure, 70 Yale L.J. 1037, 1043 (1961).

n8. La. Civ. Code art. 4.

n9. Frederick Pollock, Essays in Jurisprudence and Ethics 85 (1882).

n10. Gilmore, supra note 7, at 1043.

n11. U.C.C. section 1-103.

n12. United Nations (Vienna) Convention on Contracts for the Int'l Sale of Goods, art. 7(2).

n13. Id.

n14. Uniform Law on the International Sale of Goods art. 2.

n15. John Donne, A Selection of His Poetry 104 (Penguin ed. 1952).

n16. For explanations of differences in contract drafting, see John Langbein, Comparative Civil Procedure and the Style of Complex Contracts, 35 Am. J. Comp. L. 381 (1987); Georges A. Van Hecke, A Civilian Looks at the Common-Law Lawyer, in International Contracts: Choice of Law and Language 5, 10 (Willis L.M. Reese ed. 1962).

n17. H. Poincaré, Science and Hypothesis 89 (1952).

n18. Id.

n19. See Donne, supra note 15.

n20. Portalis et al., supra note 6.

n21. As quoted in Humphry W. Woolrych, The Life of the Right Honourable Sir Edward Coke, Knt. 197 (1826).

n22. William S. Gilbert, Iolanthe or the Peer and the Peri (Lord Mountararat's Sont) Act 2.

n23. The Louisiana Civil Code has a few definitions designated as definitions: see, e.g., La. Civ. Code art. 1756 (entitled "Obligations; definition"); La. Civ. Code art. 1763 (entitled simply "Definition" and defining a "real obligation"); La. Civ. Code art. 1825 (also entitled simply "Definition" and defining "subrogation"). Other definitions are held out as substantive rules: see, e.g., La. Civ. Code art. 1842 (entitled "Confirmation" but containing a definition of "confirmation"); La. Civ. Code art. 1843 (entitled "Ratification" but containing a definition of "ratification").

n24. A.P. Herbert, The Uncommon Law 313 (7th ed. 1950), as quoted in Hupman v. Cook, 640 F.2d 497, 504 (4th Cir. 1981).

n25. La. Civ. Code art. 1759: "Good faith shall govern the conduct of the obligor and the obligee in whatever pertains to the obligation."

n26. United Nations (Vienna) Convention on Contracts for the Int'l Sale of Goods, art. 7(2).

n27. UNIDROIT, art. 1.7.

n28. See 3 Farnsworth on Contracts section 12.4 (1990).

n29. United Nations (Vienna) Convention on Contracts for the Int'l Sale of Goods, art. 46.

n30. Id. at art. 28.

n31. UNIDROIT, art. 7.2.2.

n32. UNIDROIT, art. 7.2.2(c).

n33. UNIDROIT, art. 7.4.13.

n34. U.C.C. section 2-707 (proposed revision July 1996).

(b) *Questions*

1. How do you evaluate the practical significance of the UCC's being of interest to civil-law jurists who have "little interest in decisions of common law courts"?

2. How does the civil-law conception of legislation differ from its common-law counterpart?

3. Professor Farnsworth offers a theory to explain the greater wordiness of common-law statutes that their civil-law counterparts. Can you think of other explanations?

4. Does the common-law rejection of penalty clauses correspond to other aspects of the common-law conception of contracts?

3. *The Encounter of Legal Cultures in Judicial Applications of a Multilateral Treaty*

The passage below extends Professor Farnsworth's discussion by examining the problems of legal uniformity *after* an international convention has been drafted, and has gone into effect. Issues arise from the collision of different legal cultures when national courts seek to apply international law in a uniform way.

(a) Vivian Grosswald Curran, The Interpretive Challenge to Uniformity

15 Journal of Law and Commerce 175, 175–178 (1995)

Uniformity is a goal expressly articulated in Article 7(1) of the U.N. Convention on Contracts for the International Sale of Goods ("CISG"): "In the interpretation of this Convention, regard is to be had to its international character and to the need to promote uniformity in its application and the observance of good faith in international trade." Uniformity of application through uniformity of interpretation has become something of a sacred mission to many CISG scholars in this still embryonic stage of CISG case law development. n1 The challenges to uniformity of interpretation are, however, both formidable and numerous. They are embedded in the inevitable problems of interpretation itself, for, even within a given judicial system, uniformity of interpretation remains at best an unrealized ideal. Judges sometimes consciously sacrifice uniformity to perceived needs of justice in a pending case. Even when judges have no intention of sacrificing uniformity, however, the transmutation of an interpreted norm from precedent to pending case alters the meaning of that norm, however subtly, precluding uniformity of application.

This problem is compounded manyfold with the CISG, a written text which is to be applied in various official and unofficial language versions, n2 by courts in judicial systems as diverse as are the common and civil law systems. The difficulties of linguistic translation merge with those of different legal traditions, cultures and practices, such that concepts as basic as those of "trial" or of "contract" can have different meanings and significances at their most fundamental levels in the various legal and linguistic communities of CISG Contracting States.

Many conundrums are associated with the goal of interpreting the CISG uniformly, including what constitutes the appropriate source of legal authority to which a court should look when applying the CISG. United States judges will tend to seek authoritative guidance from the texts of prior judicial or arbitral decisions, whereas European judges will be inclined to rely far more on academic commentary. Claude Witz's book on the first judicial applications of the CISG, which might have been subtitled "or the need for judicial uniformity," should be seen in the European legal tradition of valorizing *la doctrine*, or academic commentary, as a source of law. It serves both as a retrospective assessment of the first CISG decisions and as normative prescription directed to future CISG interpretation. Indeed, his analysis of selected precedents contains a critique clearly aimed at disseminating CISG case law in a manner capable of instructing a receptive judge or arbitrator as to which aspects of precedential authority merit being followed and which are counter to the letter and/or spirit of the CISG.

His scrutiny of case law and his advocacy of a more widespread dissemination of judicial decisions to inform the opinions of Contracting State judges in their task of applying the CISG uniformly suggest the possibility that an increase in uniformity may yield a hybrid global legal system from a methodological perspective: *i.e.*, that judges in civil law countries may come to approximate their common law counterparts in increasing their reliance on precedent as a source of binding authority, while judges in common law jurisdictions may come to approximate their civil law counterparts in seeking elucidation of relevant legal principles in the explanation and critique of scholarly writing on the CISG.

Such hybridization would appear to be inevitable, at least to some extent, because common law decisions, standing independently from commentary, will be readily accessible to civil law judges. Conversely, the more cryptic style of many civil law decisions, and their publication in the context of explanatory and normative scholarly commentary, will result in common law judges understanding civil law cases through the filter, and, consequently, under the influence, of scholarly commentary. Moreover, the directive in Article 7(2) that "questions concerning matters governed by this Convention which are not expressly settled in it are to be settled in conformity with the general principles on which it is based" evokes the typical civil law interpretive methodology with respect to codes, and underscores the importance of commentary. Since one of the traditional tasks of civil law scholarly commentary is to identify the underlying principles, the crucial role of commentators in interpreting the CISG is implicit in Article 7(2) of the CISG.

Thus, one fascinating result of the substantive internationalization of the law of sales may be a concomitant unifying influence on the disparate methodological approaches of the Contracting States. Militating against this theory, however, is the possibility that their legal culture and tradition may lead civil law judges to insist on considering precedents only with accompanying scholarly commentary. As long as there continue to be few common law decisions applying the CISG, it is likely that such commentary will exist for most common law precedents.

The growing body of CISG scholarship with the conscious objective of promoting uniformity of application by disseminating information about precedents, appears to promote common law methodology by advocating attention to precedents as a source of legal authority. Paradoxically, however, it simultaneously undermines common law methodology by situating the dissemination of precedents exclusively in a context of scholarly commentary. On the other hand, if CISG case law proliferates to the extent that it becomes impossible to find commentary for common law decisions, the substantive independence of common law court opinions will enable civil law judges to rely on their own interpretations of common law precedent, without reference to commentary, resulting in a modified civil law tradition, embracing the common law characteristic of applying precedents without necessary or frequent reference to commentary.

NOTES

n1. Reported CISG case law currently is estimated at between 150 and 200 decisions, although an elusive system of case reporting in many of the signatory states virtually assures the existence, unknown to the public, of many more unpublished cases decided pursuant to the CISG. See MICHAEL R. WILL, CISG: THE U.N. CONVENTION ON CONTRACTS FOR THE INTERNATIONAL SALE OF GOODS, INTERNATIONAL BIBLIOGRAPHY, 1980–1995; THE FIRST 150 OR SO DECISIONS, 1988–1995 (1995).

n2. Professor Harry Flechtner has developed this thesis in Sources of Textual Non-Uniformity in the U.N. Sales Convention: The Several CISGs, Address to the Third International Workshop on a Legal Expert System for the U.N. Convention for the International Sale of Goods (CISG), Washington, DC, May 20, 1995. See also BIANCA & BONELL, Commentary on the International Sales Law: The 1980 Vienna Sales Convention 807 n. ("Unofficial German translation was agreed between the Governments of Austria, the Federal Republic of Germany, the German Democratic Republic and Switzerland. The Austrian, GDR, and Swiss versions contain slight differences on minor points..."). I am grateful to Professor Flechtner for bringing this passage to my attention in the context of a discussion about the many variations of the CISG, some official and some unofficial, and the attendant heightened difficulty of achieving uniformity of interpretation.

(b) *Questions*

1. How might a civil-law judge apply precedential authority in a manner more reminiscent of civil-law adjudication than of traditional common-law adjudication?

2. From the standpoint of comparative legal analysis, what are the concealed dangers that multilateral treaties may pose?

3. In which ways is it likely that the CISG will cause the civil- and common-law judicial methodologies to blend, and in which ways is it likely that the distinctive judicial methodologies will resist blending?

VII. Future Directions of Comparative Law

1. *Introduction*

This section presents conclusions, and suggests ideas for moving comparative law forward as the field enters a new century and millennium.

2. *Truths Without Truth*

(a) Vivian Grosswald Curran, *Cultural Immersion*
46 American Journal of Comparative Law 43, 83–92

VII. Conclusions

A. Of Difference and Sameness

My vision of comparative law through cultural immersion does not amount to a focus on difference for the sake of difference, and it includes the need for vigilance in preventing the recognition of difference from degenerating into a repudiation of the different, a need the generation of émigré comparatists understood so well. Appreciating each legal culture according to that culture's own perspective implies a readiness to concede that the standards by which one measures law and legality in one's own culture need not be universally valid, and that the acculturation one has received in one's own system colors and limits one's vision and understanding. Immersion comparison need not imply pervasive difference at a most fundamental level. What it does imply is the need to be open to all differences beneath the surface, and even in spite of surface similarities, as well as the possibility of differences at the most fundamental level. n141

The tension between assumptions of sameness versus difference pervades the legal field. We struggle today with deciding if laws and legal arguments should be gender and color-blind, at the risk of failing to validate circumstances and characteristics unique to women and racial minorities, and consequently placing members of those groups at a legally sanctioned disadvantage; in the alternative, if laws and legal arguments should make gender and color distinctions, or if to do so will perpetuate dangerous stereotypes of inequality. Those contemporary American legal theories, such as feminist and critical race theory, that have brought these issues to the attention of American law schools, share origins of marginalization, exclusion and exile with comparative law and with the émigré comparitists in the United States. n142 They not only emanate from, and reflect, marginalized populations, but also generally suffer from marginalization within the academic curriculum of law schools. The insights they have provided into the constitution of our legal system stem in part from the greater facility that an outside observer may have in detecting features of a legal culture so entrenched and unquestioned as to be taken for granted by the insiders. Noting the signal triumphs of the exiled, Edward Saïd has referred to "an ascetic code of willed homelessness," and Julia Kristeva has evoked exile as an opportunity to "make love with absence," and as a "weightlessness in the infinity of cultures and legacies [that] gives [the exiled] the extravagant ease to innovate." n143 This perhaps is the condition to which the comparatist should aspire.

The question remains as to whether a premise of fundamental human sameness is a prerequisite to social and legal tolerance. The debate over the philosophical sources of exclusionary ideologies has particular contemporary relevance in the international arena in the context of current ideas of multiculturalism, as well as the development of the European Union. n144 It has similarly crucial contemporary relevance in the domestic arena in the context of marginalized populations within our legal culture. The critical issue of whether an appreciation and celebration of differences among cultures corollates with bigotry and exclusion has no bearing of course on whether fundamental differences in fact exist among humans and human cultures. n145 My aim is not to promote a search for differences, or to advocate the converse of the Zweigert and Kötz approach by presuming difference. Rather, I am anxious for comparatists to beware of avoiding truths and the complexities of truths, of losing the gist of attributes of other legal cultures by overlooking the untranslatables, and of rendering themselves unable to see differences for fear of the consequences of such vision.

Entrenched categorizations that lead to presumptions of similarity are dangerous in my opinion because they stand in the way of understanding foreign legal cultures. As long as comparatists fail to identify and challenge unjustified presumptions, mistakes will be made and perpetuated, precluding both effective cultural immersion and the benefits of intercultural translations. Mistaken conclusions of similarity will not enhance understanding, and efforts to build bridges among peoples will be more, not less, doomed, as foreign legal systems continue to surprise and baffle us, diminishing mutual sympathy and respect. n146

The search for human uniformity is also a search for universality. Universal uniformity of human attributes would justify universally applicable legal principles. The problems of an *a priori* assumption of universal uniformity that does not allow for contrary findings are many. Among others, this approach may lead comparatists to advocate principles as universal which cannot withstand fluctuations over time within a given legal culture. Principles which one inadvisedly touts as universal may well be used in another place or another time for a contrary purpose, turning the original meaning of those principles on their heads. The attempt to congeal current thinking for posterity's application tends to backfire over time as theory undergoes the phenomenon Balkin calls "ideological drift," where shifts over time cause a given practice or belief to lose its original valence on the political spectrum, sometimes eventually yielding a diametrically opposite political valence. n147 One observes, thus, that differences not only divide legal cultures among nations, but also distinguish a given society in one era from another era.

The inclination to reject the possibility of irreconcilable differences at a fundamental level also is part of a far more widespread phenomenon than a reaction to fascism. It is as broad as the human urge for certainty, and the concomitant discomfort with uncertainty, with loose ends that cannot be tied. n148 The urge for certainty goes hand in hand with the urge to objectify and scientize law, and with a refusal of the disorder of complication, of irreconcilables. Scientizers have proceeded by raising the dual specters of nihilism and relativism as the alternatives to law as scientifically objective. The zeal for certainty, fuelled by normative rather than substantive arguments, often prevails, however, at the expense of truth. n149

A first step for comparative legal analysis today would seem to lie in rejecting the underlying categorizations of sameness/inclusion and difference/exclusion. Disentangling those underlying associations would obviate the need for engaging in the ultimately hopeless task of redefining apparent difference as sameness. If comparative legal analysis can achieve this dissociation, it will become free of the pervasive, entrenched substructural categorization that has manifested itself in an unwarranted focus on universal uniformity. The dissolution of what has until now been an unchallenged association underlying U.S. comparative legal analysis should facilitate heightened acuity, particularly in terms of exploring new bases for acknowledging difference while simultaneously protecting the other against discriminatory exclusion. n150

Comparative law to date has been slow to engage in the rich and fruitful discussion of differentiation versus subordination or inequality that scholars in other areas have been developing to address dilemmas raised by the law's blindness to difference. In my view, comparatists have not entered the debate because they have not yet severed the link between difference and exclusion which is a *sine qua non* of the contemporary theoretical discussion. That link may well have been forged indissolubly for those who have first-hand memories of Nazi persecution. The émigrés have much to teach us about the dangers of separating people under law, but perhaps the time has come to develop ways not merely to coexist with others, but to do so in full recognition of their difference, their *otherness*. Legal cultures that foster tolerance without uniformity, and that celebrate difference, ultimately may further the goals of the émigrés better than an *a priori* definition of all humans as fundamentally similar.

The opposing argument is that to focus on differences is to focus on particulars, and to reject normative judgment. n151 The problem of judging is, in my opinion, the most difficult issue raised by the immersion approach to comparative legal analysis. Beneficial byproducts of the immersion approach, such as humility and an increased reluctance to assume that one has exclusive propriety over absolute truth, may be distinct from a refusal to judge, but they are not calculated to encourage normative judgment.

Cultural immersion's strength is in challenging those who would base judgments on inapposite standards from the comparatist's culture of origin, and in challenging those whose assumption that their conclusions have objective validity implicitly would legitimize the imposition of one culture's standards on the practices of another. Cultural immersion does not preclude universal normative judgments in that the immersion approach merely seeks to broaden and enrich understanding. In that sense, the immersion approach should facilitate the acquisition of an informed basis for developing judgments by obliging comparatists to enhance and clarify their vision as a prerequisite to judging. Nevertheless, cultural immersion's militating against judging legal cultures by standards external to themselves inevitably challenges the legitimacy of any criticism of, or interference with, foreign cultures.

Cultural immersion thus resolves only the second of twin dangers which threaten comparative legal analysis: on the one hand, a total abdication of judgment and, on the other, the unwarranted imposition of judgment emanating from a certainty of possessing objective truth. Immersion analysis requires the individual comparatist to struggle over whether and when normative judgments are applicable or desirable. Cultural immersion is a necessary alternative to oversimplification and inaccuracy, but it does not resolve the dilemma of judging. The modernist danger of abdicating value judgment is worth taking seriously in a century that has witnessed the Soviet gulag and the Nazi concentration camp.

Martha Nussbaum has expressed optimism as to the possibility of judging other cultures without an *a priori* devalorization of their identifying attributes. She refers to "natural human practices [as being] full of moral argument and moral stand-taking..." n152 and argues against the postmodernist tendency to eschew judgment. According to Nussbaum, postmodernists unwittingly echo the philosophy of the ancient skeptics in rejecting difficulty, or what she describes as "the disturbance of compassion." n153 Nussbaum criticizes observers who refuse to judge, describing them as flawed by "the absence of an important ingredient of humanity." n154 She states that "there are ethical standards that are independent of the norms and traditions of a particular culture, n155 and underscores the dilemma: "It is important for oppressed groups who fare badly in their traditions to be able to appeal to something that is not only outside of unreflective opinion, but also 'outside' of their history and practices..." n156 Nussbaum does not explain how the irreconcilable aspects of seeking to analyze the different from within (*i.e.*, cultural immersion), and judging the other, can be harmonized so as to legitimize judgment. The closest she comes is her suggestion that the postmodernist view suffers from absolutism: that postmodernists, like the ancient skeptics, unreasonably and unnecessarily require universal acceptance of values as "the criterion of acceptability for a normative principle." n157

I do not know if Nussbaum's optimism is justified. I am inclined to be less optimistic, but I believe that Nussbaum elucidates the relation of cultural immersion to judging: namely, that both are necessary, and that these two complex and perilous tasks, while in my view not entirely reconcilable, nevertheless are also not entirely irreconcilable. n158 There are no theoretical formulas for engaging in both simultaneously. The answer, if one can call it an answer, lies in what Nussbaum refers to as natural human practices of compassion and ethical commitment. If the latter are practiced in a context of cultural immersion, perhaps the resulting judgments can better avoid or mitigate some of the excesses that historically have been associated with a certainty of possessing truth, while also avoiding an abdication of political action on behalf of oppressed minorities.

B. Of Immersion and Incommensurability

The seeming paradox of this article is that the immersion approach, with its focus on difference, implies incommensurability, and consequently the failure of comparison. It implies incommensurability, however, only in an ultimate sense. Just as communication cannot reach perfection, so comparison cannot be conducted to perfection. First, some dross from the comparatist's own legal culture will affect the interpretive process, marring total immersion. n159 Secondly, root differences between the observed culture and the comparatist's culture of origin will elude complete explanation in the terms of the comparatist's culture of origin, precisely because crucial terms of the foreign culture find no exact parallels in those of the comparatist's culture. On the other hand, the process of translating begins at this point, both betraying the original as the comparatist seeks to reveal it, but also revealing the original, as ill-fitting terminology nevertheless renders some idea of the new and different, and allows for one to start a guided imaginative act, to start to penetrate the other legal culture.

On one level, all comparison, like all translation, seeks commonalities in that it is only by means of shared terms that foreign ones can be introduced and recognized. The search to find only commonality at an underlying level, however, is an undertaking ultimately dependent on repression and bias, neither of which is likely to enhance clarity of vision or effective interaction. It may be hoped that decoupling the link between sameness and inclusion, and asserting differences where they are observed among legal cultures, even at a fundamental level, need not increase or intensify conflict.

It may, rather, cast the problems to be resolved into the public arena where they can be studied and negotiated unencumbered by an unspoken agenda, and more amenable to yielding constructive resolutions.

The incommensurability implicit in the idea of cultural immersion would only be an absolute incommensurability in a world of absolutes, a world of comparables versus incomparables. The immersion approach rejects the absolutist mentality. It contemplates a slow pushing against cultural barriers towards an ideal of mutual comprehension, a striving to approach comprehension, and a recognition that some distances will remain. Rather than failure, it implies the need to accept that others have different truths. The more deeply one gains insights into the particularities of foreign legal cultures, influenced by the flavors of each country's habits, history, language, preoccupations and social circumstances, the more aware the comparatist becomes of irreducible incomparables. Insights into particularities of identity, and the limits of comparative possibilities, of great importance in grasping foreign legal cultures, depend on a comparative framework. Such bridging of distances as we are likely to realize will entail mutual transformations in the process of comprehension. The increased acquaintance with foreign legal cultures that is cultural immersion's hallmark will result in an enhanced ability to realize the difference between the familiar and the inevitable. Such a use of comparative legal analysis can enable comparatists to penetrate to the deepest substructural levels of legal cultures, to the processes of categorization that are unarticulated and sometimes unconscious. Cultural immersion allows for both the perception and challenging of what previously has been taken for granted as necessary.

Since accepting the idea of human plurality and difference also applies to differences within legal cultures, the obstacles to successful immersion and to successful comparison are different in degree, but not in kind, among different communities within a single nation's legal culture, and among legal cultures of different nations. n160 Comparative law, when conducted effectively, should thus be an instructive model for all legal analysis. Ultimately, comparatists translate. Their renditions of foreign legal cultures are their masterpieces, reflecting at once the depth of their penetration into other legal cultures as well as the degree of their skill in reformulating the foreign into the familiar, so that those who are within the comparatists' culture of origin may gain access to the worlds of those who are not.

NOTES

n141. This last point is especially important in areas of the law in which practical results that seem the same in fact are not, because of profound differences in the respective legal systems that amount to highly different results, despite superficial appearances to the contrary. See supra n. 93.

n142. For a study of the experience of exile for intellectuals from Hitler's Europe, including an analysis of the impact on refugees of loss of native language, see Donald Peterson Kent, The Refugee Intellectual (1953). For a poignant description of Rabel's marginalization in the United States, see Großfeld & Winship, "Der Rechtsgelehrte in der Fremde," 183–200 in Der Einfluß, especially the subsection entitled "Wir wußten nicht, wer er war," at 189–90. Rabel was able to obtain only the position of Research Associate, although younger scholars who had emigrated earlier fared better.

n143. Kristeva, supra n. 13, at 10, 32. Cf. Vilem Flusser, Bodenlos: Eine Philosopische Autobiographie 252 (1992). Flusser's exile was involuntary at first, as he emigrated to Brazil as a refugee from Hitler. He describes his initial alienation as changing into a freedom peculiar to the migrant, and he presents the nomadic existence as philosophically desirable because perpetuating continual transformations in perspectives. See also Flusser, "Interview, Graz, 1990," in Zweigespräche. Interviews 1967–1991 (1996); and Gertrude Stein, An American in France (1936). (The point of having roots is to take them with one.)

n144. See Samuel P. Huntington, The Clash of Civilizations and the Remaking of World Order (1996) (The post-cold war world will see conflict among political ideologies give way to conflicts of cultures, with culture defined in part in terms of ethnic homogeneity.); and Gibson & Caldeira, "The Legal Cultures of Europe," 30 Law & Soc'y Rev. 55, 80 (1996) ("we fully expect that differences in legal cultures will play an even greater role in the ways in which EC law gets implemented within each of the member states.")

n145. See Weiler, supra n. 119, for a most thoughtful and subtle handling of this question in the context of the European Union. Weiler posits that community and belongingness must imply exclusion, yet advocates full freedom of cultural diversity in the nations of the EU because of the apparent widespread depth of the human longing for both cultural uniqueness and group belonging. The result need not, in his view, be a sacrifice of civil and political rights of foreigners within the various nation states. It will be, rather, a European Union that tolerates cultural and ethnic diversity while standardizing political rights, and that separates the ideas of nation and state. See also George F. Kennan, At a Century's Ending: Reflections 1982–1995, 11 (1996) (attributing the problems of the United Nations to its failure to distinguish between nation and state). Cf., Legrand, "Legal Traditions in Western Europe: The Limits of Commonality," in R. Jagtenberg et al., Transfrontier Mobility of Law 67 (1995) (Loss of pluralism in Europe is necessary price of integration).

n146. Cf. Rodolfo Sacco, in Legrand, supra n. 48, at 949 ("The comparatist's teach ing necessarily favors some values. But only the comparatist who cheats establishes in advance which values will be prioritized.") For a nuanced, complexity-welcoming approach, see Grobetafeld, supra n. 99. Großfeld's comparative approach strikes me both as entirely appropriate and highly humane. He recommends building bridges by appreciating commonalities among different legal cultures, prefacing his remarks, how ever, with a discursus on the need for comparatists to search for reality, rather than for what their particular cultures and training have prepared them to expect to find. His emphasis on commonalities emanates from a humanistic tradition fortified, I would suggest, by the effect of the holocaust on contemporary legal culture, and on German legal culture in particular. His caution against complacently confusing what we see with reality seems to me to provide a theoretical component that the emigre comparatists tended to neglect or at the least to leave unarticulated. The beauty of approaches such as Großfeld's in my opinion is that they tally with what I see as the goal of comparative legal analysis, and, on another level, of all legal analysis: trans muting and translating the unknown, the different, the other into the familiar. See also Sturm, "Sameness and Subordination: The Dangers of a Universal Solution," 143 U. Pa. L. Rev. 201 (1994) for an excellent discussion of the dangers of insisting on sameness as a predicate for judicial inquiry; and Minow, supra n. 1.

n147. See Balkin, "The Footnote," 83 N.W.U.L. Rev. 275 (1989) (Shift over time from formerly liberal to currently conservative political valence of strict judicial scrutiny of civil rights, and judicial deference to congressional acts in area of economic rights.); and Balkin, "Ideological Drift and the Struggle Over Meaning," 25 Conn. L. Rev. 869 (1993). See also Rawls, supra n. 73 (Legal bases can be transitory).

n148. See e.g., Erich Fromm, Escape from Freedom (1967); and Erich Fromm, The Sane Society (1955).

n149. See Curran, supra n. 65, at 19–24. Indeed, as Steven Winter has pointed out, the postmodernist predicament is neither nihilism nor relativism, but "too many [foundations] with...a resulting profusion of meaning...leading to problems of decidability." Winter, supra n. 64, at 42. See Fromm, supra n. 148, on the irreconcila ble human desires for freedom and security. See also Giambattista Vico, "Principi di scienca nuova," in Opere, ed. Fausto Nicolini (1953) bk. I, XLVII at 452 ("The human mind naturally tends to delight in the uniform.") quoted in Pierre Legrand, Comparatists-At-Law and the Contrarian Challenge (Inaugural Lecture, 20 October 1995, manuscript on file with the author); and Goodrich, supra n. 4, at 20 (typically, the English doctrinal premise has been that "inconsistencies and contradictions in [the common law] are quite simply unthinkable, they are...failures of understanding and not of law"); and Gordley & Mattei, "Protecting Possession," 44 Am. J. Comp. L. 293 (1996) (for an illustration in the area of property law of legal rationalizations in Ger many, France and England to avoid acknowledging such "failures of law").

n150. See Sturm, supra n. 146, at 212 on the precariousness of depending on findings of sameness ("Those who make and enforce the rules can determine when to expose and act on the difference that we knew was there all along."); de Varennes, supra n. 2, at 111 (governmental impositions of an official language may be motivated by goal of treating all citizens equally, but result in exclusionary discrimination). See also Minow, "Interpreting Rights: An Essay for Robert Cover," 96 Yale L.J. 1860, 1871 (1987) (Describing the danger of "fitting women's claims, for example, into an equality framework that makes sameness to man a prerequisite [because this] may distort or deny the importance of differences."); MacKinnon, supra n. 1, at 4 (differentiation as a distinct concept from equality); and Colker, supra n. 2, at 1033 (proposing that courts require evidence of subordination for a prima facie case of race or sex discrimination, and that evidence solely of differentiation be deemed insufficient for a prima facie case.).

n151. See Minow & Spelman, "In Context," 63 S. Cal. L. Rev. 1597, 1630–31. Accord Finkielkraut, supra n. 105.

n152. Nussbaum, "Valuing Values: A Case for Reasoned Commitment," 6 Yale J.L. & Hum. 197, 208 (1994).

n153. Id. But see Cornell, "Post-Structuralism, the Ethical Relation, and the Law," 9 Cardozo L. Rev. 1587, 1590 (1988) (far from being unconcerned with ethics, postmodernists as insist on the ethical). My own view is somewhere between Cornell's and Nussbaum's. I do not see postmodernists as refusing the difficulties and disturbances of complexity when they decline to judge the other. My sense is, rather, that, paradoxically, while claiming to reject absolutism, they approach the issue of judgment in an absolutist manner, and conclude that judgment lacks legitimacy be cause it cannot be derived logically from postmodernist premises. The irony here lies in postmodernism's inability to espouse its own tenets, for, as Winter writes in defense of postmodernism, "it is...the insistence on...the absolute that is both nihilist and profoundly antihumanist." Winter, supra n. 64, at 245.

n154. Id.

n155. Id. at 214.

n156. Id. at 214. But cf. Schlag, "Values," 6 Yale J.L. & Hum. 219, 225 (1994) (" 'Values' are the secular equivalent of God— they are the continuation of theology by other means.") Cf. also Emmanuel Levinas' analysis of charity and justice: "Does not the essential difference between charity and justice come from the preference of charity for the other, even when, from the point of view of justice, no preference is any longer possible?" Levinas, supra n. 115, at 84.

n157. Nussbaum, id. at 206. More cautiously optimistic is Changeux, who believes that the mutual impenetrability of cultures impedes the possibility of universals in ethics. Along Kantian lines, however, he states that the urge to be ethical is a human universal, and that, therefore, ethics proceeds from the very fact of society." Changeux, supra n. 14, at 216. Cf. Habermas, "Struggles for Recognition in the Democratic Constitutional State," in Multiculturalism, 107, 125–26 (Amy Gutmann; ed. Shierry Weber Nicholsen, trans. 1994) ("What sets off the battles is not the ethical neutrality of the legal order but rather the fact that every legal community and evey democratic process for actualizing basic rights is inevitably permeated by ethics.")

n158. Cf. Taylor, "The Politics of Recognition," in Multiculturalism, id., at 69 ("If the judgment of value is to register something independent of our own wills and desires, it cannot be dictated by a principle of ethics....One doesn't, properly speak ing, make judgments that can be right and wrong; one expresses liking or dislike, one endorses or rejects another culture. But then ...the validity or invalidity of judgments [is no longer the question]").

n159. It is in this sense that George Steiner writes that "there are no translations." Steiner, supra n. 6, at 270. Steiner nevertheless also believes that there are great translations. He defines the latter as "not an equivalence, for there can be none, but a vital counterpoise, an echo, faithful yet autonomous, as we find in the dialogue of human love. Where it fails, through immodesty or blurred perception, it traduces. Where it succeeds, it incarnates." Id. at 270–71.

n160. Julia Kristeva has even analyzed an irreconcilable plurality of discourses within each individual. She applies psychoanalytic theory in a fascinating study in which she concludes that the rejection of the other emanates from the discomfort people feel with a sense of foreignness within themselves. According to Kristeva, the path to accepting the different in others lies in acknowledging the strangers within ourselves. See Kristeva, supra n. 13, at 1, 191. ("Delicately, Freud does not speak of foreigners: he teaches us how to detect foreignness in n. 115, at 82 ("The relationship with the other, taken at the level of our civilization, is a complication of our relation ship [with the other in ourselves]."). The French philosopher Vladimir Jankélévitch was of the view that "it is minimal otherliness which engenders the most inexpiable hatreds, feeds the most tenacious rancors...."; Vladimir Jankélévitch & Béatrice Berlowitz, Quelque part dans l'inachevé 62 (1978).

(b) *Questions*

1. What is the importance for comparative legal analysis of entrenched customs and associations?

2. What examples of "ideological drift" have occurred in the United States, resulting in shifting political valence of substantive positions?

3. How might comparative law assist in illustrating the battleground between a desire for certainty and security, and a desire for freedom and change?

4. Should comparative law eschew all normative evaluations?

Acknowledgments

Permission to print or reprint was granted by the copyright owners as follows:

The American Journal of Comparative Law for excerpts from Vivian Grosswald Curran, *Cultural Immersion, Difference and Categories in US. Comparative Law* (1998).

The Journal of Law and Commerce for the excerpt from Vivian Grosswald Curran, The Interpretive Challenge to Uniformity (1995).

University of Pennsylvania Law Review for excerpts from William Ewald, *Comparative Jurisprudence I: What Was It Like to Try a Rat?* (1995).

Louisiana State University Law Review for the excerpt from E. Allan Farnsworth, *A Common Lawyer's View of His Civilian Colleagues* (1996).

AMS Press (republished 2d edition—exact replica) for the excerpts from Lon Fuller, THE LAW IN QUEST OF ITSELF (1940).

Mohr Siebeck for the excerpts from Bernhard Großfeld, KERNFRAGEN DER RECHTSVERGLEICHUNG (1996) (as translated into English by Vivian Grosswald Curran).

Blanche Grosswald for the excerpts from Blanche Grosswald, *The Right to Physician-Assisted Suicide* (originally published in present volume).

Index of Names

Index of Words